Canadian Living's best PASTA

BY

Elizabeth Baird

AND

The Food Writers of Canadian Living Magazine
and The Canadian Living Test Kitchen

A MADISON PRESS BOOK
PRODUCED FOR
BALLANTINE BOOKS AND CANADIAN LIVING™

Ballantine Books
A Division of
Random House of
Canada Limited
1265 Aerowood Drive
Mississauga, Ontario
Canada
L4W 1B9

Canadian Living
Telemedia
Communications Inc.
50 Holly Street
Toronto, Ontario
Canada
M4S 3B3

Canadian Cataloguing in Publication Data

Pasta

(Canadian Living's best)
ISBN 0-345-39795-9

1. Cookery (Pasta).   I. Baird, Elizabeth.
II. Series.
TX809.M17P3 1994   641.8'22   C94-930273-2

**Produced by
Madison Press Books
40 Madison Avenue
Toronto, Ontario
Canada
M5R 2S1**

Printed in Canada

Contents

Introduction 5

Pasta Shapes 6

Presto Pastas 8

Wok, Pot and Skillet 40

Great Bakes 50

Long Simmers 66

Magnifico Salads 74

Making Fresh Pasta 86

Credits 88

Index 90

Introduction

We're all marching to the drum of time and convenience these days. And the ingredient that's right in step with us is pasta.

Today old standbys like macaroni, spaghetti and flat noodles have been joined by radiatore, penne and farfalle, words that fall off our tongues as easily as if we were saying radiators, pens and bow ties. And fresh pasta, the dinner-party rage of a decade ago, has stayed on so deliciously that spinach fettuccine is now as available in supermarkets as bags of P.E.I potatoes.

What's the cornerstone of pasta's popularity? First of all, it's so easy. Boil the pasta in a big pot of water, toss with a sauce, and presto, supper's ready. But pasta is more than just easy. It's also very satisfying, a real crowd-pleaser, and kids adore it, the simpler the better. Drizzled with tomato sauce and sprinkled with cheese, pasta is always a fail-safe supper.

Pasta can also trace its roots back to the Orient where it is found in a host of Chinese, Thai and Japanese dishes. Fast-laners call it their own when topped with five-minute mushroom sauces or tossed with a stir-fry. Sophisticated palates love to dress it up with funky goat cheese and sun-dried tomatoes or sauce it with rich Gorgonzola or smoky salmon strips and lemon.

As if this weren't enough, pasta is also inexpensive. And it plays an important role in a healthful diet. In the new *Canada's Food Guide to Healthy Eating,* pasta belongs to the top category of foods we should be eating.

For all of these reasons — and more — we proudly present *Canadian Living's Best Pasta,* bringing you everything from quick suppers to simmering sauces and splendid salads. In all, you'll find more than 100 new ways to serve delicious and pleasing pasta to family and friends.

Elizabeth Baird

*Capellini with Smoked Salmon
and Lemon Cream Sauce (p. 32)*

TORTELLINI

SPINACH LASAGNA

LASAGNA

THIN CHINESE
WHEAT NOODLES

FUSILLI LUNGHI

TUBETTI

CURLY CHINESE
WHEAT NOODLES

MACARONI

ROTELLI

DITALI

FETTUCCINE

WHOLE WHEAT
SPAGHETTI

CAPELLINI

SPAGHETTINI

LINGUINE

FARFALLE

RIGATONI

FETTUCCINE

STELLINI

RICE VERMICELLI

FUSILLI

RADIATORE

PENNE

RICE STICK
NOODLES

CHINESE WHEAT
NOODLES

ROTINI

BUCATINI

VERMICELLI

MEDIUM
CONCHIGLIE

SOBA

JUMBO
CONCHIGLIE

MEDIUM
EGG
NOODLES

Presto Pastas

No wonder pasta is so popular — it cooks up quickly, tosses with almost any combination of ingredients and is ready in no time at all!

Summer-Fresh Pasta ▶

A quick mushroom sauté joins with fresh basil and ripe tomatoes in this simplest of all pasta sauces. Vary the sauce to suit your taste with extras such as slivered black olives, fresh parsley and chives. Or, choose fresh oyster or shiitake mushrooms for extra flavor.

1/3 cup	extra virgin olive oil	75 mL
1	onion, chopped	1
3	cloves garlic, minced	3
2 cups	sliced mushrooms (about 8 oz/250 g)	500 mL
1/4 tsp	dried thyme	1 mL
3/4 tsp	salt	4 mL
1/2 tsp	pepper	2 mL
12 oz	linguine or spaghetti	375 g
4 cups	chopped tomatoes (about 4)	1 L
1/2 cup	chopped fresh basil	125 mL
	Freshly grated Parmesan cheese	
	Fresh basil leaves	

● In skillet, heat 2 tbsp (25 mL) of the oil over medium heat; cook onion and garlic, stirring, for 3 minutes or until softened.

● Add mushrooms, thyme, salt and pepper; cook, stirring, for about 5 minutes or until mushrooms are softened, adding up to 1/4 cup (50 mL) water to prevent sticking.

● Meanwhile, in large pot of boiling salted water, cook linguine for 8 to 10 minutes or until tender but firm; drain well. Toss with mushroom mixture, tomatoes, remaining oil and chopped basil. Sprinkle with Parmesan to taste; garnish with basil leaves. Makes 4 servings.

TIP: For a delicious summer salad, cool the pasta mixture to room temperature; toss with 1 tbsp (15 mL) balsamic or red wine vinegar.

Puttanesca with Linguine

Once popular with streetwalkers (puttanesca), this quickly made chunky combination of tomatoes, garlic, olives and capers is now a lusty pasta classic.

2 tbsp	olive oil	25 mL
4	cloves garlic, minced	4
1/2 cup	each sliced Kalamata and pimiento-stuffed olives	125 mL
2 tbsp	drained capers	25 mL
1/4 tsp	each dried oregano, salt and hot pepper flakes	1 mL
1	can (19 oz/540 mL) tomatoes	1
1/4 cup	chopped fresh parsley	50 mL
	Pepper	
12 oz	linguine	375 g
	Freshly grated Parmesan cheese	

● In skillet, heat oil over medium heat; cook garlic, Kalamata and pimiento-stuffed olives, capers, oregano, salt and hot pepper flakes, stirring occasionally, for 3 minutes.

● Mash tomatoes with juice; add to skillet and bring to boil. Reduce heat and simmer for about 10 minutes or until thickened. Stir in parsley. Season with pepper to taste.

● Meanwhile, in large pot of boiling salted water, cook linguine for 8 to 10 minutes or until tender but firm; drain well. Toss with sauce; sprinkle with Parmesan to taste. Makes 4 servings.

Oodles of Noodles

Kids just love pasta, especially this tomato one thickened and smoothed out with cream cheese.

1	can (28 oz/796 mL) tomatoes	1
1/2 cup	chopped onion	125 mL
1 tsp	dried basil (optional)	5 mL
1/4 tsp	(approx) pepper	1 mL
4 oz	light cream cheese, cubed	125 g
2-3/4 cups	macaroni or fusilli	675 mL
1/4 cup	freshly grated Parmesan cheese	50 mL
	Salt	

● In saucepan, bring tomatoes, onion, basil (if using) and pepper to boil; reduce heat and simmer for 15 minutes.

● Pour into food processor or blender; purée. Add cream cheese; purée until smooth.

● Meanwhile, in large pot of boiling salted water, cook macaroni for 8 to 10 minutes or until tender but firm; drain well. Toss with sauce; sprinkle with Parmesan. Season with salt and pepper to taste. Makes 8 servings.

Fresh Tomato and Basil Toss

Please don't make this sauce unless it's tomato and fresh basil season. The charm of a quick toss of hot pasta and uncooked tomatoes depends on the robust flavor of sun-ripened tomatoes.

4 cups	diced seeded tomatoes	1 L
1/2 cup	chopped fresh basil	125 mL
1/4 cup	extra virgin olive oil	50 mL
1 tsp	red wine vinegar	5 mL
3	cloves garlic, minced	3
1 tsp	salt	5 mL
1/2 tsp	pepper	2 mL
4 cups	rotini or penne	1 L
	Freshly grated Parmesan cheese	

● In bowl, combine tomatoes, basil, oil, vinegar, garlic, salt and pepper. *(Tomato mixture can be covered and set aside for up to 1 hour.)*

● In large pot of boiling salted water, cook rotini for 8 to 10 minutes or until tender but firm; drain well. Toss with tomato mixture; sprinkle with Parmesan to taste. Makes 4 servings.

TIP: Never store tomatoes in the refrigerator. The cold deadens their flavor.

Arrabbiata

Feisty is the best way to describe both the sauce and its name!

1 tbsp	olive oil	15 mL
1	onion, chopped	1
1	zucchini, diced	1
1	carrot, diced	1
1	sweet red pepper, diced	1
1/2 tsp	hot pepper flakes	2 mL
1/2 tsp	salt	2 mL
1/4 tsp	pepper	1 mL
1	can (28 oz/796 mL) tomatoes, mashed	1
12 oz	spaghetti	375 g
2 tbsp	chopped fresh parsley	25 mL
	Freshly grated Parmesan cheese	

● In large skillet, heat oil over medium heat; cook onion, zucchini, carrot, red pepper, hot pepper flakes, salt and pepper for about 5 minutes or until softened.

● Pour in tomatoes; bring to boil. Reduce heat and simmer for 10 to 15 minutes or until thickened.

● Meanwhile, in large pot of boiling salted water, cook spaghetti for 8 to 10 minutes or until tender but firm; drain well. Toss with sauce and parsley; sprinkle with Parmesan to taste. Makes 4 servings.

Ditali in Tomato Chick-Pea Sauce

2 tbsp	olive oil	25 mL
3 cups	sliced mushrooms (12 oz/375 g)	750 mL
2	cloves garlic, minced	2
1	onion, finely chopped	1
1	can (14 oz/ 398 mL) chick-peas, drained and rinsed	1
1	can (28 oz/796 mL) tomatoes, chopped	1
3/4 tsp	salt	4 mL
1/2 tsp	each pepper and dried oregano	2 mL
1-3/4 cups	ditali, penne or macaroni	425 mL
2 tbsp	chopped fresh parsley	25 mL
1/4 cup	freshly grated Parmesan cheese	50 mL
	Parsley sprigs	

● In large skillet, heat oil over medium-high heat; cook mushrooms, garlic and onion, stirring occasionally, for 10 to 15 minutes or until liquid has evaporated and mushrooms are browned.

● Stir in chick-peas, tomatoes, salt, pepper and oregano; bring to boil. Reduce heat and simmer rapidly for about 5 minutes or until slightly thickened.

● Meanwhile, in large pot of boiling salted water, cook ditali for 8 to 10 minutes or until tender but firm; drain well. Toss with sauce and parsley. Arrange on warmed serving platter; sprinkle with Parmesan. Garnish with parsley sprigs. Makes 4 servings.

Ditali (thimbles) are short and stubby, a perfect match for a meatless sauce studded with chunky chick-peas.

Creamy Leek Fettuccine

2	leeks	2
5	slices bacon, chopped	5
1/2 tsp	dried thyme	2 mL
1-1/2 cups	half-and-half cream	375 mL
2 oz	light cream cheese, cubed (1/4 cup/50 mL)	50 g
1 tsp	Dijon mustard	5 mL
1 tsp	pepper	5 mL
1/2 tsp	salt	2 mL
12 oz	fettuccine or linguine	375 g
	Parsley sprigs	

● Trim leeks and cut in half lengthwise; spread leaves and rinse thoroughly under cold water to flush out grit. Cut crosswise into thin slices.

● In skillet, cook one-quarter of the bacon over high heat until crisp; set aside for garnish. Reduce heat to medium; cook remaining bacon for 4 minutes or until limp. Drain off all but 1 tbsp (15 mL) fat.

● Add leeks and thyme; cook, stirring occasionally, for about 5 minutes or until softened. Add cream, cream cheese, mustard, pepper and salt; bring to boil, stirring to melt cheese.

● Meanwhile, in large pot of boiling salted water, cook fettuccine for 8 to 10 minutes or until tender but firm; drain well. Toss with sauce. Arrange on warmed serving platter; garnish with reserved bacon and parsley. Makes 4 servings.

Leeks are definitely the classy member of the onion family, but don't let the lack of leeks prevent you from trying this recipe. Just substitute two large onions and you have a delicious new variation. Cheaper, too.

CLEANING LEEKS

Since the best part of a leek is the white part, growers hill earth up around the leek as it develops in order to keep out the light and get as much white as possible. As a result, leeks harbor a lot of grit that must be removed before using.
● To clean leeks, trim off coarse outer leaves and trim down to just above the green part. Slit through the outer layers of the leek right down to the root end. Holding leeks by the root end, swish them in water, running cold water through the layers to remove dirt.

Red Pepper Herb Pasta

To go from a vegetable pasta dish to a vegetarian one, simply substitute vegetable stock for the chicken stock.

2	sweet red peppers	2
1/2 cup	chicken stock	125 mL
1/4 cup	(approx) freshly grated Parmesan cheese	50 mL
2 tbsp	cream cheese	25 mL
4 tsp	olive oil	20 mL
1/4 tsp	pepper	1 mL
Pinch	hot pepper flakes (optional)	Pinch
2 tbsp	each chopped fresh basil, parsley and oregano	25 mL
1 lb	fettuccine	500 g

● Broil red peppers, turning often, for about 20 minutes or until blistered and charred. Let cool, then peel off blackened skin; cut in half, core and seed.

● In food processor, purée red peppers, chicken stock, Parmesan, cream cheese, oil, pepper, and hot pepper flakes (if using) until smooth. Pour into saucepan; cook over medium heat for about 5 minutes or until heated through. Stir in basil, parsley and oregano.

● Meanwhile, in large pot of boiling salted water, cook fettuccine for 8 to 10 minutes or until tender but firm; drain well. Toss with sauce; sprinkle with more Parmesan to taste. Makes 4 to 6 servings.

Tomato, Eggplant and Artichoke Spaghetti

Eggplant adds a rich taste and texture, almost meaty in nature, to the vegetarian sauce. For the photo, we used cavatappi, a corkscrew spaghetti.

1	eggplant (about 1 lb/500 g)	1
1 tsp	(approx) salt	5 mL
2 tbsp	olive oil	25 mL
1/2 cup	sliced black olives	125 mL
1	onion, chopped	1
1	jar (6 oz/170 mL) marinated artichokes, drained and sliced	1
1 tbsp	capers	15 mL
2	cloves garlic, minced	2
1 tsp	dried oregano	5 mL
1/4 tsp	hot pepper flakes	1 mL
4	tomatoes, peeled, seeded and chopped	4
3 tbsp	tomato paste	45 mL
1/4 cup	chopped fresh parsley	50 mL
	Pepper	
1 lb	spaghetti	500 g
1/4 cup	freshly grated Parmesan cheese	50 mL

● Cut eggplant into 1/2-inch (1 cm) cubes. In colander, sprinkle eggplant with salt. Let stand for 30 minutes. Rinse and pat dry.

● In large heavy saucepan, heat oil over medium heat; cook olives, onion, artichokes, capers, garlic, oregano and hot pepper flakes, stirring, for 4 minutes or until onion is softened.

● Stir in eggplant, tomatoes and tomato paste; cover and cook, stirring often, for about 15 minutes or until eggplant is tender and sauce has thickened. Stir in parsley, and salt and pepper to taste.

● Meanwhile, in large pot of boiling salted water, cook spaghetti for 8 to 10 minutes or until tender but firm; drain well. Toss with sauce; sprinkle with Parmesan. Makes 4 to 6 servings.

(clockwise from top) Zucchini Carrot Pasta (p. 14); Tomato, Eggplant and Artichoke Spaghetti; Red Pepper Herb Pasta.

Zucchini Carrot Pasta

Two stars from the summer garden team up with pretty bow-tie pasta for a dish that's ready in minutes (photo, p. 13).

2 tbsp	olive oil	25 mL
1 cup	chopped red onion	250 mL
3	cloves garlic, minced	3
3 cups	each sliced carrots and zucchini	750 mL
1 cup	vegetable stock	250 mL
8 cups	farfalle	2 L
1 cup	freshly grated Parmesan cheese	250 mL
1/2 tsp	pepper	2 mL
	Salt	
1/4 cup	each chopped fresh parsley and basil	50 mL

● In skillet, heat oil over medium-high heat; cook onion and garlic, stirring, for about 3 minutes or until softened.

● Add carrots; cook, stirring, for 2 minutes. Add zucchini; cook, stirring, for 3 minutes. Pour in stock and bring to boil; cook for 2 minutes.

● Meanwhile, in large pot of boiling salted water, cook farfalle for 8 to 10 minutes or until tender but firm; drain and return to pot. Stir in vegetable mixture, Parmesan, pepper, and salt to taste. Gently toss with parsley and basil. Makes 6 servings.

Olive and Sun-Dried Tomato Spaghettini

The success of this simple pasta toss depends on the best olive oil (see sidebar, p. 19) and black olives. Avoid canned black olives; they're too bland. Instead, choose black olives with oomph — available in bulk in Italian, Greek and Portuguese grocery stores as well as in some specialty shops and supermarkets.

1 lb	spaghettini	500 g
1/2 cup	extra virgin olive oil	125 mL
4	cloves garlic, minced	4
1/4 tsp	hot pepper flakes	1 mL
1/2 cup	black olives, cut into large pieces	125 mL
1/4 cup	drained oil-packed sun-dried tomatoes, cut into strips	50 mL
1 tsp	salt	5 mL
1/4 tsp	pepper	1 mL
1/4 cup	chopped fresh basil or parsley	50 mL

● In large pot of boiling salted water, cook spaghettini for 8 to 10 minutes or until tender but firm; drain well.

● Meanwhile, in large skillet, heat half of the oil over medium heat; cook garlic and hot pepper flakes for 2 to 3 minutes or until fragrant but not browned.

● Add olives, tomatoes, salt and pepper; cook for 2 to 3 minutes or until heated through. Add to pasta along with remaining oil and basil; toss well. Makes 6 servings.

TIP: If sun-dried tomatoes are unavailable, substitute 3/4 cup (175 mL) chopped fresh tomatoes and cook them with the garlic and hot pepper flakes for 3 to 4 minutes before adding the olives.

OLIVES

● Olives are picked either unripe (green), almost ripe (red to black), or ripe (black). They are virtually inedible until they are cured. Commercial methods of curing olives include soaking them in olive oil, water, brine or salt for several months; dry-curing them in salt; or lye-curing them in a strong alkaline solution and then rinsing thoroughly, which is the most common method used.

● Whenever possible, taste olives before you buy them. In grocery stores specializing in foods from Greece, Italy and the Middle East, olives are often sold in bulk in bins. Most shopkeepers offer samples to buying customers.

● Choose from tangy pointy purple Kalamata olives, mellower dry-cured black olives which are excellent for cooking, tiny Niçoise olives packed in olive oil and jumbo greens so beloved for snacking.

● Supermarkets provide choices, too, especially in jarred olives, but avoid canned ripe olives — they get the prize for bland!

Kasha and Bows ▲

1/3 cup	butter	75 mL
2	onions, chopped	2
1 cup	kasha	250 mL
1	egg, beaten	1
2 cups	boiling water	500 mL
1 tsp	salt	5 mL
1/4 tsp	pepper	1 mL
4 cups	farfalle or macaroni	1 L

● In skillet, melt butter over medium heat; cook onions for 10 to 15 minutes or until browned and crisp.

● Meanwhile, in saucepan, cook kasha with egg over medium heat, stirring, for about 2 minutes or until kasha seems dry. Add water, salt and pepper; reduce heat, cover and simmer for about 10 minutes or until kasha is tender and liquid is absorbed.

● Meanwhile, in large pot of boiling salted water, cook farfalle for 8 to 10 minutes or until tender but firm; drain well and toss with kasha and onions. Makes 6 servings.

TIP: Adding an egg to the kasha before it is cooked separates the grains and gives a nice texture.

Kasha (hulled kernels of buckwheat) tossed with farfalle doubles as a satisfying main dish or side dish. For our photograph, we used red onions and cooked them until tender but not browned.

Penne with Swiss Chard, Raisins and Pine Nuts ▲

Both *Swiss chard and rapini, if you prefer it, have a pleasant bitterness that's perfectly in balance with the sweetness of raisins and the meatiness of pine nuts.*

1 lb	Swiss chard (or rapini)	500 g
1/3 cup	extra virgin olive oil	75 mL
1	onion, chopped	1
3	cloves garlic, minced	3
3/4 tsp	salt	4 mL
1/2 tsp	pepper	2 mL
Pinch	hot pepper flakes	Pinch
1/2 cup	raisins	125 mL
1 tbsp	balsamic or red wine vinegar	15 mL
4 cups	penne	1 L
1/3 cup	toasted pine nuts	75 mL

● Separate Swiss chard into ribs and leaves; cut into 1-inch (2.5 cm) pieces. In large pot of boiling salted water, cook Swiss chard ribs for 7 minutes. Add leaves and cook for 3 minutes. Drain and refresh under cold water. Drain and set aside.

● In large skillet, heat oil over medium heat; cook onion, garlic, salt, pepper and hot pepper flakes for 5 minutes or until softened. Add Swiss chard, raisins and vinegar; toss together.

● Meanwhile, in large pot of boiling salted water, cook penne for 8 to 10 minutes or until tender but firm. Drain and toss with Swiss chard mixture. Garnish with pine nuts. Makes 4 servings.

Tomato and Eggplant Whole Wheat Spaghetti

1	eggplant (about 1 lb/500 g)	1
1 tsp	salt	5 mL
4 tsp	vegetable oil	20 mL
1	large onion, chopped	1
2	cloves garlic, minced	2
2 tbsp	water	25 mL
1	can (28 oz/796 mL) tomatoes, crushed	1
2 tsp	dried basil	10 mL
Pinch	hot pepper flakes	Pinch
	Salt and pepper	
12 oz	whole wheat spaghetti	375 g
2 tbsp	chopped fresh parsley	25 mL
2 tbsp	freshly grated Parmesan cheese	25 mL

● Cut eggplant into 1/2-inch (1 cm) cubes. In colander, sprinkle eggplant with salt. Let stand for 30 minutes. Rinse and pat dry.

● In saucepan, heat oil over medium-high heat; cook eggplant, stirring, for 2 minutes. Add onion, garlic and water; cook for 3 minutes.

● Add tomatoes, basil and hot pepper flakes; bring to boil. Reduce heat and simmer for 20 to 30 minutes or until thickened and eggplant is tender. Season with salt and pepper to taste.

● Meanwhile, in large pot of boiling salted water, cook spaghetti for 8 to 10 minutes or until tender but firm; drain well. Toss with sauce, parsley and Parmesan. Makes 4 servings.

Eggplant may seem like an ordinary vegetable until you taste what it does to a simple tomato sauce — adding a satisfying meatiness that the basil and hot pepper flakes accent.

Creamy Rotini with Asparagus

1 lb	fresh asparagus	500 g
1/4 cup	butter, melted	50 mL
1	clove garlic, minced	1
2	shallots, finely chopped	2
1 cup	whipping cream	250 mL
3/4 cup	creamy goat cheese (chèvre), cubed	175 mL
1 tsp	grated lemon rind	5 mL
2 tbsp	lemon juice	25 mL
	Salt and pepper	
4 cups	rotini or penne	1 L
1/4 cup	freshly grated Parmesan cheese	50 mL
1/4 cup	slivered black olives	50 mL
3	green onions, sliced	3

● Snap tough ends off asparagus and discard; cut stalks diagonally into 1-inch (2.5 cm) pieces. In saucepan, bring 1/2 cup (125 mL) water to boil; add asparagus and cook for 2 to 3 minutes or until tender-crisp. Drain well and set aside.

● In saucepan, heat 2 tbsp (25 mL) of the butter over medium heat; cook garlic and shallots for about 2 minutes or until softened. Add cream and bring to boil; reduce heat to simmer.

● Whisk in goat cheese, lemon rind and juice until smooth. Season with salt and pepper to taste. Stir in asparagus; cook until heated through.

● Meanwhile, in large pot of boiling salted water, cook rotini for 8 to 10 minutes or until tender but firm; drain well. Toss with remaining butter; toss with sauce. Transfer to warmed serving platter; sprinkle with Parmesan, olives and green onions. Makes 8 appetizer servings.

Asparagus stars in an easy springtime appetizer. You can omit the olives and use one small onion instead of the shallots.

New-Style Pasta Primavera

In this nineties version of a pasta classic, the whipping cream has been abandoned in favor of lots of herbs, lemon juice and quick cooking which retains flavors and textures.

2 tbsp	butter	25 mL
2	cloves garlic, minced	2
2	zucchini, chopped	2
2	carrots, chopped	2
1	sweet red pepper, chopped	1
1	onion, cut into thin wedges	1
1 lb	asparagus or broccoli, cut into 1-1/2-inch (4 cm) pieces	500 g
1-1/2 cups	peas	375 mL
1 cup	canned chicken broth (undiluted)	250 mL
3 tbsp	each chopped fresh chives and oregano	50 mL
1 tsp	salt	5 mL
3/4 tsp	pepper	4 mL
12 oz	fusilli lunghi	375 g
1/2 cup	freshly grated Parmesan cheese	125 mL
2 tbsp	chopped fresh parsley	25 mL
1 tbsp	lemon juice	15 mL

● In large skillet, melt butter over medium heat; cook garlic, zucchini, carrots, red pepper, onion and asparagus, stirring occasionally, for 3 minutes.

● Add peas, chicken stock, chives and oregano; bring to boil. Reduce heat and simmer for 5 minutes or until vegetables are tender-crisp. Stir in salt and pepper.

● Meanwhile, in large pot of boiling salted water, cook fusilli for 8 to 10 minutes or until tender but firm; drain well. Toss with vegetable mixture. Sprinkle with Parmesan and parsley; toss again. Sprinkle with lemon juice; toss again. Makes 4 to 6 servings.

Aglio e Olio

Garlic and olive oil create all the sauce you need for this traditional old-country pasta. This is one recipe where the quality of the olive oil really counts (see sidebar, next page).

1/2 cup	extra virgin olive oil	125 mL
8	cloves garlic, minced	8
1 tsp	salt	5 mL
1/2 tsp	hot pepper flakes	2 mL
12 oz	spaghetti	375 g
1/3 cup	chopped fresh parsley	75 mL
	Pepper	

● In small saucepan or skillet, heat oil over low heat; cook garlic, salt and hot pepper flakes, watching carefully and stirring occasionally, for about 15 minutes or until garlic is light golden but not browned.

● Meanwhile, in large pot of boiling salted water, cook spaghetti for 8 to 10 minutes or until tender but firm; drain well.

● Toss with oil mixture and parsley. Season with pepper to taste. Makes 4 servings.

VARIATION

TOASTED CRUMBS AND GARLIC: Reduce hot pepper flakes to 1/4 tsp (1 mL). Coarsely crumble enough crustless Italian or French bread to make 2 cups (500 mL) fresh crumbs. Toast in 350°F (180°C) oven for 8 minutes or until crisp and golden. Prepare Aglio e Olio as above, adding crumbs to pasta along with oil mixture.

Presto Pesto

2 cups	packed fresh basil leaves	500 mL
1/2 cup	freshly grated Parmesan cheese	125 mL
1/4 cup	pine nuts	50 mL
3/4 cup	extra virgin olive oil	175 mL
3	cloves garlic, minced	3

● In food processor, finely chop basil, Parmesan and pine nuts.

● With motor running, gradually add oil in thin steady stream. Stir in garlic. Makes 1 cup (250 mL).

TIP: It's always a good idea to save a little of the pasta cooking water to thin out the pesto as you are tossing it with the pasta.

August is the time to whirl up batches of pesto and freeze them in containers just the right size for a bowl of pasta. This recipe makes enough to toss with about 1-1/2 lb (750 g) long pasta and serve six.

OLIVE OILS

Buying olive oil can be confusing — so many types from so many countries and for such a price range. Here are a some suggestions that will help you make the right choice.

● All olive oil is made from olives, the fruit of the olive tree, and most come from countries around the Mediterranean where olives have been cultivated for about 6,000 years.

● Oil released from the first grinding and pressing of olives is superior — fruitier, more robust and low in acid. Look for **extra virgin** on the label for this oil but note that, even among the extra virgin bottles, which must have less than 1% acidity, differences in quality exist. Some producers blend oils to lower the acid level of their lesser-quality oil, enabling these bottles to be labeled "extra virgin" as well.

● The best advice is to look for the words "**cold pressed**" or "**first cold pressing**" when looking for **quality extra virgin olive oil**. Understandably, this cold-pressed oil is more expensive, but it is an oil you use sparingly, reserving it for pasta dishes such as Aglio e Olio (p. 18) or Presto Pesto (this page) where the taste and presence of the olive oil really matter. Use it, too, for dressing salads and cooked vegetables, dipping crusty sourdough bread or as a table condiment.

● Lower in price is **pure olive oil**, made from the second or third pressing of the olives. This rather bland oil has been treated to lower its acid level, and lacks the characteristic olive flavor and color. However, it can be used in frying or in any dish where you want a neutral oil.

● So-called "**light**" **olive oil** is not lighter in calories, simply lighter in color and flavor.

● Store unopened olive oil in a dark, cool place for up to 2 years. Once opened, use up the bottle within 2 months, storing it as before.

Mushroom Tofu Noodles ▲

A *warm golden egg noodle, available fresh in Oriental grocery stores, tastes terrific with this vegetarian topping, but other pasta types such as fusilli taste just fine, too. Toasting the almonds adds so much oomph to the dish that you shouldn't miss that step.*

1 tbsp	vegetable oil	15 mL
2	cloves garlic, minced	2
1	large onion, chopped	1
3 cups	thinly sliced mushrooms (12 oz/375 g)	750 mL
Half	each sweet red and green pepper, diced	Half
1/2 cup	vegetable stock	125 mL
1/4 cup	tamari or soy sauce	50 mL
1 tsp	ginger	5 mL
2 tsp	cornstarch	10 mL
1 lb	firm tofu, grated	500 g
1	pkg (350 g) steamed Chinese noodles	1
1/2 cup	slivered almonds, toasted (see TIP, p. 25)	125 mL
4	green onions, chopped	4

● In skillet, heat oil over medium heat; cook garlic and onion for about 3 minutes or until softened.

● Stir in mushrooms, red and green peppers, stock, tamari and ginger until coated. Reduce heat and simmer, covered, for about 5 minutes or until mushrooms are softened.

● Blend cornstarch with 1 tbsp (15 mL) water; stir into skillet. Mix in tofu; cover and simmer for about 5 minutes or until heated through.

● Meanwhile, in large pot of boiling salted water, cook noodles for about 2 minutes or until tender but firm; drain well. Arrange on warmed serving platter. Top with tofu mixture; sprinkle with almonds and green onions. Makes 4 servings.

Linguine with Wild Mushroom Sauce

1/2 oz	dried porcini mushrooms	15 g
1 tbsp	butter	15 mL
1	onion, chopped	1
3	cloves garlic, minced	3
1/2 tsp	dried thyme	2 mL
1/2 tsp	salt	2 mL
1/4 tsp	pepper	1 mL
1 cup	sliced fresh mushrooms (4 oz/125 g)	250 mL
1 cup	whipping cream	250 mL
1/4 cup	freshly grated Parmesan cheese	50 mL
12 oz	linguine	375 g

● Rinse dried mushrooms under cold water. Soak for 15 minutes in 1/2 cup (125 mL) boiling water. Strain through cheesecloth-lined sieve, reserving liquid. Rinse mushrooms; chop coarsely.

● In skillet, melt butter over medium heat; cook onion, garlic, porcini mushrooms, thyme, salt and pepper for 3 minutes or until softened.

● Add fresh mushrooms and reserved soaking liquid; cook for 2 minutes. Pour in cream and bring to boil; boil for 2 minutes or until slightly thickened. Remove from heat; stir in Parmesan.

● Meanwhile, in large pot of boiling salted water, cook linguine for 8 to 10 minutes or until tender but firm; drain well. Toss with sauce. Makes 4 servings.

Porcini mushrooms, available dried in delis and Italian grocery stores, deliver such a wonderful cascade of taste with each bite that they're worth every penny for this special-occasion pasta.

Saucy Parmesan Pasta with Asparagus

1 lb	fresh asparagus	500 g
2 tbsp	butter	25 mL
1/3 cup	chopped green onions	75 mL
2 tbsp	all-purpose flour	25 mL
1/4 tsp	each pepper and nutmeg	1 mL
1-3/4 cups	milk	425 mL
3/4 cup	freshly grated Parmesan cheese	175 mL
12 oz	fusilli or penne	375 g

● Snap tough ends off asparagus and discard; cut stalks diagonally into 1-inch (2.5 cm) pieces. In saucepan, bring 1/2 cup (125 mL) water to boil; add asparagus and cook for 2 to 3 minutes or until tender-crisp. Drain well and set aside.

● In same saucepan, melt butter over medium heat; cook onions, stirring, for 3 minutes or until softened. Stir in flour, pepper and nutmeg; cook for 1 minute. Gradually whisk in milk until smooth; cook, whisking, for 3 to 5 minutes or until boiling and thickened. Stir in Parmesan until melted.

● Meanwhile, in large pot of boiling salted water, cook fusilli for 8 to 10 minutes or until tender but firm; drain well. Toss with sauce and asparagus. Makes 4 servings.

VARIATION

SAUCY CHEDDAR PASTA: Substitute Cheddar cheese for the Parmesan. Season with salt and pepper to taste.

The base of this pleasing dish is a cream sauce accented with nutmeg.

Gourmand's Gorgonzola Linguine

Indulgent, special-occasion, worth every last calorie! — they all apply to this creamy, cheesy sauce.

12 oz	linguine or spaghetti	375 g
1 cup	whipping cream	250 mL
1 tbsp	butter	15 mL
6 oz	Gorgonzola cheese, crumbled	175 g
1/4 cup	(approx) freshly grated Parmesan cheese	50 mL
1/2 tsp	(approx) pepper	2 mL
	Salt	

● In large pot of boiling salted water, cook linguine for 8 to 10 minutes or until tender but firm; drain well.

● Meanwhile, in heavy saucepan, bring cream and butter to boil; boil for 1 minute. Reduce heat to low; stir in Gorgonzola until melted. Stir in Parmesan and pepper; toss with pasta.

● Arrange on warmed serving platter; sprinkle with more Parmesan, salt and pepper to taste. Makes 4 servings.

Fettuccine Alfredo — The Classic

For some reason, this is a favorite party dish for kids. It must be the meltingly mild and smooth sauce with a hint of nutmeg — the same reason adults can't wait to dig into a bowl of classic Alfredo!

12 oz	fettuccine	375 g
1 cup	whipping cream	250 mL
1/4 cup	butter	50 mL
1 cup	freshly grated Parmesan cheese	250 mL
1/2 tsp	salt	2 mL
1/4 tsp	pepper	1 mL
Pinch	nutmeg	Pinch
	Parsley sprigs	

● In large pot of boiling salted water, cook fettuccine for 8 to 10 minutes or until tender but firm; drain well.

● Meanwhile, in large saucepan or skillet, bring cream and butter just to boil. Reduce heat and stir in Parmesan, salt, pepper and nutmeg; toss with pasta. Arrange on warmed serving platter; garnish with parsley. Makes 4 servings.

THE BEST CHEESES FOR PASTA

Cheeses with character and/or creaminess are the best matches for pasta. Old Cheddar, Gruyère, Emmenthal, Gorgonzola, feta and creamy goat cheese (chèvre) all add enough distinctly robust taste to carry off pasta's background blandness. Here's more on some of the most popular cheeses for pasta.

● **Parmesan**: Parmigiano Reggiano is the authentic grainy cheese from the area around Parma, Italy. Although it is more expensive than its imitators, a little of its magnificent full taste goes a long way. A wedge of it keeps in the refrigerator for weeks, at the ready to grate over pasta. Avoid pre-grated Parmesan as it is usually dry and often acrid.

● **Mozzarella**: This ivory-colored unripened cheese gives creaminess and stretch, especially to baked pastas where other stronger ingredients make up for its mildness.

● **Provolone**: A stretchy cheese that starts out mild with a bit of an edge but becomes strong, tangy and robust as it ages, provolone blends well with other cheeses and gives depth to their flavor.

● **Ricotta**: This soft and moist, slightly granular unripened cheese has a milky taste and comes in varying degrees of milk fat. It is often used in stuffed or baked pasta, and is sold in tubs, like yogurt or sour cream.

● **Asiago**: This sharp hard cheese is wonderful shaved over pasta. Use as you would Parmigiano Reggiano.

● **Pecorino Romano**: Grate this pungent cheese over pasta and to make a crusty top on baked pasta dishes. Use as you would Parmigiano Reggiano.

Alfredo's Leaner Fettuccine

12 oz	fettuccine or linguine	375 g
1 cup	2% cottage cheese	250 mL
1/3 cup	freshly grated Parmesan cheese	75 mL
1/4 cup	2% milk	50 mL
1/4 tsp	each salt and pepper	1 mL
Pinch	nutmeg	Pinch
	Parsley sprigs	

● In large pot of boiling salted water, cook fettuccine for 8 to 10 minutes or until tender but firm; drain well and return to pot.

● Meanwhile, in food processor, purée cottage cheese until smooth. Add Parmesan, milk, salt, pepper and nutmeg; blend until smooth.

● Add to drained pasta; cook over medium heat, stirring constantly, for 1 minute. Arrange on warmed serving platter; garnish with parsley. Makes 4 servings.

While special occasions let us indulge, everyday eating should be as lean as possible. Here's how Canadian Living's Test Kitchen trimmed off fat and calories from the classic Alfredo, and still came up with a wonderfully satisfying and great-tasting dish.

Instant Mac and Cheese

1-1/2 cups	macaroni	375 mL
1 cup	shredded Cheddar cheese	250 mL
1/4 cup	plain yogurt	50 mL
1 tbsp	butter	15 mL
1 tbsp	Dijon mustard	15 mL
1/4 tsp	each salt and pepper	1 mL
Pinch	hot pepper flakes	Pinch

● In large pot of boiling salted water, cook macaroni for about 8 to 10 minutes or until tender but firm; drain well.

● Meanwhile, in bowl, stir together Cheddar and yogurt; set aside.

● In same pot over low heat, melt butter; stir in mustard, salt, pepper and hot pepper flakes. Add macaroni and toss to coat. Remove from heat; add cheese mixture and toss. Makes 2 servings.

You know those boxed macaroni and cheese suppers that are ready so fast and are so good for filling tummies? Well, this one takes only seconds longer to prepare — and tastes much, much better. You'll never go back to boxed again!

Macaroni with Four Cheeses

3/4 cup	shredded mozzarella cheese	175 mL
3/4 cup	shredded Cheddar cheese	175 mL
3/4 cup	shredded Gruyère cheese	175 mL
1/3 cup	freshly grated Parmesan cheese	75 mL
2-3/4 cups	macaroni	675 mL
3/4 cup	light cream	175 mL
	Chopped fresh parsley	
	Pepper	

● In bowl, combine mozzarella, Cheddar, Gruyère and half of the Parmesan; set aside.

● In large pot of boiling salted water, cook macaroni for 8 to 10 minutes or until tender but firm; drain well and return to pot.

● Add cheese mixture and cream; cook over low heat for 1 minute or until cheese has melted. Sprinkle with remaining Parmesan, and parsley to taste. Season with pepper to taste. Makes 4 servings.

Mozzarella gives you lusciously gooey stretch, Cheddar and Parmesan touch the flavor high notes and Swiss Gruyère fills in the mellow background.

Garden-Fresh Spaghetti ▼

Chopped sweet pepper and tomatoes, added at the end of the cooking time, give the beef sauce freshness and crunch.

1 tbsp	vegetable oil	15 mL
1 lb	ground beef	500 g
1	onion, chopped	1
Half	stalk celery, diced	Half
3	cloves garlic, minced	3
1	can (28 oz/796 mL) tomato sauce	1
1-1/2 tsp	each dried basil and oregano	7 mL
1/2 tsp	salt	2 mL
Pinch	pepper	Pinch
2	tomatoes, chopped	2
1	sweet yellow, red or green pepper, diced	1
1 lb	spaghetti	500 g
1 cup	shredded mozzarella cheese	250 mL
1/4 cup	freshly grated Parmesan cheese	50 mL

● In large deep skillet, heat oil over medium heat; cook beef, onion, celery and garlic, stirring, for 5 minutes or until meat is browned. Drain off fat.

● Add tomato sauce, basil, oregano, salt and pepper; bring to boil. Reduce heat, cover and simmer for 15 minutes. Stir in tomatoes and sweet pepper.

● Meanwhile, in large pot of boiling salted water, cook spaghetti for 8 to 10 minutes or until tender but firm; drain well. Toss with sauce. Sprinkle with mozzarella and Parmesan. Makes 4 to 6 servings.

Very Tomato and Chicken Ragu

1 tbsp	olive oil	15 mL
1	onion, chopped	1
2	cloves garlic, minced	2
1-1/2 tsp	dried basil	7 mL
1/2 tsp	dried oregano	2 mL
1/4 tsp	hot pepper flakes	1 mL
1 lb	ground chicken	500 g
1	can (28 oz/796 mL) tomatoes	1
1/4 cup	tomato paste	50 mL
2 tbsp	chopped sun-dried tomatoes	25 mL
1 tsp	salt	5 mL
1/4 tsp	pepper	1 mL
12 oz	spaghetti or spaghettini	375 g
	Freshly grated Parmesan cheese	

● In large skillet, heat oil over medium heat; cook onion, garlic, basil, oregano and hot pepper flakes, stirring, for 3 minutes or until softened.

● Add ground chicken; cook, breaking up into large chunks, for 5 to 8 minutes or until no longer pink. Drain off any fat.

● Add tomatoes, breaking up into chunks, tomato paste, sun-dried tomatoes, salt and pepper; bring to boil. Reduce heat and simmer for 20 minutes or until thickened.

● Meanwhile, in large pot of boiling salted water, cook spaghetti for 8 to 10 minutes or until tender but firm; drain well. Toss with sauce. Sprinkle with Parmesan to taste. Makes 4 servings.

Very tomato, because the sauce contains tomatoes three ways — canned, paste and sun-dried.

Chicken Curry Pasta

2 tbsp	vegetable oil	25 mL
2	cloves garlic, minced	2
1	onion, chopped	1
1 tbsp	curry powder	15 mL
1/4 tsp	each paprika and ginger	1 mL
1 lb	boneless skinless chicken breasts, slivered	500 g
1-1/4 cups	chicken stock	300 mL
2 tbsp	tomato paste	25 mL
1/3 cup	raisins	75 mL
1/3 cup	plain yogurt	75 mL
1/2 tsp	salt	2 mL
1/4 tsp	pepper	1 mL
4 cups	penne	1 L
1/4 cup	chopped fresh coriander or parsley	50 mL
1/4 cup	chopped peanuts or almonds, toasted (see TIP below)	50 mL

● In large skillet, heat oil over medium-high heat; cook garlic and onion for 2 minutes or until softened. Add curry powder, paprika and ginger; cook, stirring, for 1 minute. Add chicken; cook, stirring, for 3 minutes or until lightly browned.

● Stir in 1/4 cup (50 mL) of the stock; cook for 1 minute or until evaporated. Add remaining stock and tomato paste; bring to boil. Reduce heat and sprinkle with raisins; simmer for 5 minutes or until chicken is no longer pink inside. Remove from heat; stir in yogurt, salt and pepper.

● Meanwhile, in large pot of boiling salted water, cook penne for 8 to 10 minutes or until tender but firm; drain well. Toss with sauce; arrange on warmed serving platter. Garnish with coriander and peanuts. Makes 4 servings.

Italy meets India in a deliciously different pasta dish with a spicy-sweet taste. Top each serving with a dollop of yogurt.

TIP: To toast peanuts or almonds, cook in small skillet over medium-low heat for 3 to 5 minutes or until golden.

Cheesy Chicken Fettuccine

Kids will love this mild pasta sauce. For sophisticated palates, replace most of the mozzarella with gutsier provolone.

2 tbsp	olive oil	25 mL
1 lb	boneless skinless chicken breasts, slivered	500 g
1/2 tsp	dried rosemary	2 mL
1/4 cup	chicken stock	50 mL
1 tbsp	all-purpose flour	15 mL
1-1/2 cups	milk	375 mL
1-1/2 cups	frozen peas	375 mL
1/2 cup	each shredded mozzarella and provolone cheeses	125 mL
1/4 cup	freshly grated Parmesan cheese	50 mL
1/4 cup	chopped fresh parsley	50 mL
1/4 tsp	each salt and pepper	1 mL
12 oz	fettuccine	375 g

● In large skillet, heat oil over medium-high heat; cook chicken and rosemary, stirring, for about 5 minutes or until golden brown. Remove from skillet and set aside.

● Pour stock into skillet, stirring to scrape up any brown bits; cook for about 1 minute or until reduced to 1 tbsp (15 mL).

● Sprinkle with flour; stir until smooth. Stir in milk and peas; bring to boil, stirring.

● Remove from heat; gradually whisk in mozzarella, provolone and Parmesan until smooth. Stir in chicken, parsley, salt and pepper.

● Meanwhile, in large pot of boiling salted water, cook fettuccine for 8 to 10 minutes or until tender but firm; drain well. Toss with sauce. Makes 4 servings.

Oriental Stir-Fry Pasta

Stir-fries over rice are old hat. Over pasta, they're new to us, but quite authentic. If you can find fresh Chinese noodles (available in various widths and colors), sold vacuum-packed in Oriental shops, do use them in this recipe. Since they're fresh, you'll need about 1 lb (500 g).

1	each carrot and stalk celery	1
3	boneless skinless chicken breasts	3
1 tbsp	olive oil	15 mL
1	small onion, chopped	1
2 tbsp	minced gingerroot	25 mL
2	cloves garlic, minced	2
1 cup	sliced mushrooms (4 oz/125 g)	250 mL
2 cups	trimmed snow peas	500 mL
1	sweet red pepper, cut into thin strips	1
2 tbsp	dry sherry	25 mL
1/4 cup	oyster sauce	50 mL
2 tbsp	soy sauce	25 mL
1 tsp	sesame oil	5 mL
Pinch	hot pepper flakes	Pinch
8 oz	spaghettini	250 g
1 tbsp	sesame seeds	15 mL

● Thinly slice carrot and celery on diagonal; set aside. Cut chicken into strips.

● In wok or large skillet, heat oil over medium-high heat; cook chicken, stirring, for 3 minutes or until browned. Transfer to plate and set aside.

● Add carrot, celery, onion, ginger and garlic to wok; cook, stirring, for 3 minutes or until softened. Add mushrooms; cook for 1 minute.

● Return chicken to wok along with snow peas, red pepper and sherry; cover and cook for 4 minutes or until chicken is no longer pink inside. Stir in oyster sauce, soy sauce, sesame oil and hot pepper flakes, mixing well.

● Meanwhile, in large pot of boiling salted water, cook spaghettini for 8 to 10 minutes or until tender but firm; drain well. Toss with chicken mixture; sprinkle with sesame seeds. Makes 4 servings.

Penne with Creamy Tomato Sauce

4	slices bacon, diced (about 4 oz/125 g)	4
1	onion, chopped	1
1	can (19 oz/540 mL) tomatoes	1
1/2 cup	whipping cream	125 mL
1/4 cup	vodka (optional)	50 mL
4 cups	penne	1 L
	Salt and pepper	
1/2 cup	freshly grated Parmesan cheese	125 mL

● In large saucepan, cook bacon over medium heat for 3 minutes. Add onion; cook for 2 to 3 minutes or until softened.

● Add tomatoes and mash with potato masher; bring to boil. Reduce heat and simmer for 20 minutes or until thickened slightly. Stir in cream; simmer for 5 minutes longer. Stir in vodka (if using).

● Meanwhile, in large pot of boiling salted water, cook penne for 8 to 10 minutes or until tender but firm; drain well. Toss with sauce; season with salt and pepper to taste. Sprinkle with Parmesan. Makes 4 servings.

Bacon adds a wonderful smoky flavor to this special-occasion dish.

Amatriciana

8 oz	pancetta or bacon (in one piece), diced	250 g
1	onion, chopped	1
1/2 tsp	hot pepper flakes	2 mL
1/4 tsp	each salt and pepper	1 mL
1	can (28 oz/796 mL) tomatoes, puréed	1
1/2 cup	freshly grated Parmesan cheese	125 mL
12 oz	bucatini or spaghetti	375 g
1 tbsp	chopped fresh parsley	15 mL

● In large skillet, cook pancetta over medium-low heat for about 8 minutes or until crisp; transfer to plate.

● Pour off all but 1 tbsp (15 mL) fat from skillet. Add onion, hot pepper flakes, salt and pepper; cook, stirring occasionally, for 3 minutes.

● Pour in tomatoes; return pancetta to skillet and bring to boil. Reduce heat and simmer for about 10 minutes or until thickened. Stir in half of the Parmesan.

● Meanwhile, in large pot of boiling salted water, cook bucatini for 8 to 10 minutes or until tender but firm; drain well. Toss with sauce; sprinkle with remaining Parmesan and parsley. Makes 4 servings.

TIP: Pancetta is rolled bacon that has been cured in salt and spices but has not been smoked. It's available in Italian grocery stores.

Bucatini, thick tubular spaghetti, is perfect for holding every drop of this classic zesty sauce.

WHICH PASTA IS BEST?

● When shopping for pasta, choose a product made from semolina — finely ground granules from the hardest durum wheat. Packages and ingredient lists usually indicate durum semolina or *pasta di semola di grano duro*. This pasta has a pleasant, firm bite to it and will keep its shape when cooked. It is also easier to stuff, and won't soak up excessive amounts of water, sauce or salad dressing.

● Quality pasta is not restricted to imported brands; Canadian-made pasta from hard Canadian wheat is available in supermarkets across the country.

Fettuccine with Chicken Livers

Chicken livers, ground beef, tomatoes and sweet peppers add up to a superlative and inexpensive pasta dish. Since the recipe makes a big batch of sauce, you can divide it into convenient amounts and serve on more than one occasion.

2 lb	fettuccine	1 kg
2 tbsp	butter	25 mL
1 cup	freshly grated Parmesan cheese	250 mL
1/4 cup	chopped fresh parsley	50 mL
	SAUCE	
1/4 cup	olive oil	50 mL
1	clove garlic, minced	1
1 lb	lean ground beef	500 g
1 lb	chicken livers, trimmed and diced	500 g
1	can (28 oz/796 mL) tomatoes, puréed	1
2	each sweet green and red peppers, finely chopped	2
1 tsp	salt	5 mL
1/4 tsp	pepper	1 mL

● SAUCE: In large deep skillet, heat oil over medium heat; cook garlic and beef, stirring to break up meat, until no longer pink. Add chicken livers; cook until no longer pink.

● Add tomatoes and bring to boil; reduce heat and simmer for about 30 minutes or until reduced and slightly thickened.

● Add green and red peppers, salt and pepper; cook for 15 minutes.

● Meanwhile, in large pot of boiling salted water, cook fettuccine for 8 to 10 minutes or until tender but firm; drain well and toss with butter. Add sauce and mix thoroughly. Stir in cheese and parsley; toss again. Makes 8 to 10 servings.

Spaghetti with Chicken Livers and Tomatoes

Chicken livers remain a great bargain, but that's not why you should try this recipe. Try it because the taste is authentically Italian, authentically delicious — and it takes just minutes to make! It's great with a spinach salad.

2 tbsp	vegetable oil	25 mL
1	small onion, chopped	1
3	cloves garlic, finely chopped	3
Pinch	hot pepper flakes	Pinch
8 oz	chicken livers, trimmed and diced	250 g
1	can (28 oz/796 mL) tomatoes, puréed	1
1 tsp	each salt and pepper	5 mL
1 lb	spaghetti	500 g
2 tbsp	chopped fresh parsley	25 mL

● In large deep skillet, heat oil over medium-high heat; cook onion, garlic and hot pepper flakes, stirring occasionally, for 3 to 4 minutes or until softened.

● Add chicken livers and cook until browned. Add tomatoes, salt and pepper; bring to boil. Reduce heat and simmer for 10 minutes or until thickened.

● Meanwhile, in large pot of boiling salted water, cook spaghetti for 8 to 10 minutes or until tender but firm; drain well. Toss with sauce; sprinkle with parsley. Makes 4 servings.

PASTA STORAGE

● **Dried pasta** can be stored in an airtight container or package at dry room temperature for up to 1 year.

● **Commercial fresh pasta** should be stored in the refrigerator and used by the "best before" date on the package.

● **Homemade fresh pasta** (see p. 86) is best cooked as soon as it has been made; otherwise, store in refrigerator for up to 2 days.

Or, dry at room temperature and store in refrigerator for up to 1 week.

Peas, Prosciutto and Tortellini

1 lb	frozen cheese tortellini	500 g
1 cup	ricotta cheese	250 mL
3/4 cup	milk	175 mL
2 tbsp	butter	25 mL
1/4 cup	chopped green onions	50 mL
4	slices prosciutto or ham, chopped	4
Pinch	hot pepper flakes (optional)	Pinch
2/3 cup	cooked or frozen green peas	150 mL
1/2 tsp	pepper	2 mL
Pinch	nutmeg	Pinch
	Salt	
1/4 cup	freshly grated Parmesan cheese	50 mL

● In large pot of boiling salted water, cook tortellini for about 10 minutes or until tender but firm; drain well.

● Meanwhile, in blender or food processor, purée together ricotta cheese and milk until smooth.

● In large skillet, melt butter over medium heat; cook onions, prosciutto, and hot pepper flakes (if using), stirring, for 5 minutes or until softened.

● Stir in cooked tortellini, ricotta mixture, green peas, pepper and nutmeg; cook, stirring, until heated through and tortellini are well coated. Season with salt to taste. Sprinkle with Parmesan. Makes 4 servings.

Frozen tortellini is the easy answer when you want a satisfying pasta dinner in a hurry. Here, cheese tortellini gets a quick creamy sauce studded with peas.

Penne with Sausage and Tomato

12 oz	sweet Italian sausage (about 4)	375 g
1 tbsp	olive oil	15 mL
1	onion, chopped	1
1	sweet red pepper, diced	1
1/4 tsp	hot pepper flakes	1 mL
1	can (28 oz/796 mL) tomatoes	1
1/4 tsp	each salt and pepper	1 mL
1/4 cup	chopped fresh parsley	50 mL
4 cups	penne	1 L
	Freshly grated Parmesan cheese	

● Remove casings from sausage; crumble meat. In large skillet, heat oil over medium-high heat; cook sausage, onion, red pepper and hot pepper flakes, stirring, for 5 minutes or until sausage is no longer pink.

● Drain and chop tomatoes, reserving 1/4 cup (50 mL) juice. Add tomatoes, juice, salt and pepper to skillet; bring to boil. Reduce heat and simmer for 5 to 7 minutes or until slightly thickened. Stir in parsley.

● Meanwhile, in large pot of boiling salted water, cook penne for 8 to 10 minutes or until tender but firm; drain well. Toss with sauce; sprinkle with Parmesan to taste. Makes 4 servings.

When you're looking for an ingredient that gives you flavor fast, you'll find sausage comes to the rescue quite often. Naturally, the better the sausage, the better the sauce — so it's worth finding the best maker of fresh sausages in your community.

Spaghetti Carbonara

This satisfying combo of bacon (pancetta), eggs and creamy cheese cloaking strands of spaghetti is just the dish to have in your repertoire when (a) the cupboard is pretty bare, (b) you don't have a lot of time, and (c) you and your household need a comforting dish. A green salad is nice alongside.

2 tbsp	butter or olive oil	25 mL
1	onion, chopped	1
2	cloves garlic, minced	2
4 oz	pancetta or bacon, diced	125 g
3	eggs	3
1 tsp	salt	5 mL
12 oz	spaghetti	375 g
1/2 cup	freshly grated Parmesan cheese	125 mL
2 tbsp	chopped fresh parsley	25 mL

● In small skillet, melt butter over medium heat; cook onion and garlic for 3 minutes or until softened. Add pancetta; cook, stirring occasionally, for about 6 minutes or until slightly crisp.

● In small bowl, lightly beat eggs with salt; set aside.

● Meanwhile, in large pot of boiling salted water, cook spaghetti for 8 to 10 minutes or until tender but firm. Drain and return to pot over medium heat.

● Immediately stir in Parmesan, parsley and pancetta mixture. Stir in eggs; cook, stirring, for about 30 seconds or until eggs are lightly cooked and pasta is coated. Serve immediately. Makes 4 servings.

Farfalle with Ham and Ricotta

Pasta bows show off a creamy sauce flecked with green onion and ham.

6 oz	thinly sliced Black Forest ham	175 g
1	stalk celery	1
5	green onions	5
1 tbsp	butter	15 mL
2 cups	ricotta cheese	500 mL
2 tbsp	milk	25 mL
1/4 tsp	dried sage	1 mL
Pinch	nutmeg	Pinch
1/2 cup	freshly grated Parmesan cheese	125 mL
	Salt and pepper	
6 cups	farfalle	1.5 L

● Slice ham and celery into thin strips, about 1-1/2 inches (4 cm) long and 1/4 inch (5 mm) wide. Cut onions in half lengthwise; cut into 1-1/2-inch (4 cm) long strips.

● In skillet, melt butter over medium-high heat; cook ham, celery and onions, stirring occasionally, for 5 to 7 minutes or until vegetables are softened and just beginning to brown.

● Add ricotta, milk, sage and nutmeg; reduce heat to medium-low and cook, stirring, until warmed through (cheese will still appear curdy). Stir in Parmesan, and salt and pepper to taste.

● Meanwhile, in large pot of boiling salted water, cook farfalle for 8 to 10 minutes or until tender but firm; drain well. Toss with sauce. Makes 4 servings.

TIP: Avoid powdered sage since it gives a fusty, tired taste to any dish it touches. Instead, dry your own bunches of fresh sage and crumble for sauces like this one, or buy crumbled sage in bottles at the supermarket.

Shrimp and Vegetable Pasta ▲

3/4 cup	chicken stock	175 mL
1	onion, chopped	1
1	carrot, thinly sliced	1
3	cloves garlic, minced	3
1/4 tsp	each salt and pepper	1 mL
6 oz	large shrimp, peeled and deveined	175 g
2 cups	broccoli florets	500 mL
1	sweet red pepper, diced	1
2 tbsp	chopped fresh dill	25 mL
1 tsp	Worcestershire sauce	5 mL
4 oz	linguine or spaghetti	125 g
1/3 cup	freshly grated Parmesan cheese	75 mL

● In skillet, bring stock to boil; add onion, carrot, garlic, salt and pepper. Reduce heat and simmer for 5 minutes.

● Add shrimp, broccoli and red pepper; return to boil. Reduce heat and simmer, covered, for 3 to 5 minutes or until shrimp are pink and broccoli is tender-crisp. Stir in dill and Worcestershire sauce.

● Meanwhile, in pot of boiling salted water, cook linguine for 8 to 10 minutes or until tender but firm; drain well. Arrange on plates; sprinkle with half of the Parmesan. Top with shrimp mixture; sprinkle with remaining Parmesan. Makes 2 servings.

P*asta is a wonderful solution when serving one or two. Cooking the toppings all together also cuts out mess and fuss.*

Capellini with Smoked Salmon and Lemon Cream Sauce

There's no fooling this time. Whipping cream is at the heart of this lemon-accented sauce — a whole cupful (250 mL)! — and it's definitely a special-occasion dish. (See photo, p. 4.)

1 cup	whipping cream	250 mL
1 tsp	grated lemon rind	5 mL
1/2 tsp	salt	2 mL
1/4 tsp	white pepper	1 mL
6 oz	smoked salmon, cut into 1/2-inch (1 cm) wide strips	175 g
1 cup	frozen peas	250 mL
12 oz	capellini or spaghettini	375 g
2 tbsp	butter	25 mL
2 tbsp	lemon juice	25 mL
2 tbsp	chopped green onion	25 mL

● In saucepan, bring cream to boil; stir in lemon rind, salt and pepper. Reduce heat and simmer gently, stirring occasionally, for 5 minutes or until thickened slightly. Stir in salmon and peas; cook for 1 minute.

● Meanwhile, in large pot of boiling salted water, cook capellini for 6 to 8 minutes or until tender but firm; drain well. Toss with butter, lemon juice and sauce. Sprinkle with green onion. Makes 4 servings.

Easy Tuna and Garlic Pasta

This is a gutsy pasta, probably more for adults than kids, and ideal for a quick supper. If time is short, use thawed frozen spinach, making sure all the excess liquid is pressed out before chopping. Pasta shells (conchiglie) catch the chunky sauce nicely.

1	pkg (10 oz/284 g) fresh spinach, trimmed	1
1/4 cup	extra virgin olive oil	50 mL
1	onion, chopped	1
4	cloves garlic, minced	4
1/3 cup	chopped fresh basil or parsley	75 mL
1 tsp	each salt and pepper	5 mL
4 cups	conchiglie or rotini	1 L
2	cans (each 7-1/2 oz/213 mL) tuna, drained and broken into chunks	2

● Rinse spinach; shake off excess water. In saucepan, cook spinach, with just the water clinging to leaves, over high heat for 1 to 2 minutes or until wilted. Drain and let cool slightly; squeeze out excess liquid. Chop coarsely and set aside.

● In skillet, heat oil over medium-low heat; cook onion and garlic for 5 minutes or until softened. Add spinach, basil, salt and pepper; cook, stirring, for 2 minutes or until heated through.

● Meanwhile, in large pot of boiling salted water, cook conchiglie for 8 to 10 minutes or until tender but firm; drain well. Lightly toss with spinach mixture, then tuna. Makes 4 servings.

BUYING AND PREPARING MUSSELS

● Mussels must be alive when purchased. Gathered wild mussels have shells that are tightly closed, but the shells of cultivated mussels, the kind now most available at fish counters, tend to gape. Test each mussel individually, tapping it lightly. Alive mussels close up quickly. Those that remain open should be avoided.

● Just to be sure, hold each closed mussel between your thumb and forefinger, pressing the shells gently on the bias. If the shell opens, the mussel is dead.

● To keep mussels alive until cooking time, transfer them as soon as possible from store wrappings to bowl. Cover with wet cloth and store in refrigerator. Do not cover mussels with water.

● As close as possible to cooking time, scrub mussels with a stiff brush under cold running water. Pull beard back while cutting it off with a knife or mussel shell.

Fusilli with Mussels ▲

2 lb	mussels	1 kg
2 tbsp	olive oil	25 mL
1	onion, chopped	1
4	cloves garlic, thinly sliced	4
1 cup	clam juice	250 mL
1 tsp	dried thyme	5 mL
1/4 tsp	hot pepper sauce	1 mL
1	can (19 oz/540 mL) tomatoes, drained and chopped	1
2 tbsp	butter	25 mL
1/3 cup	chopped fresh parsley	75 mL
	Salt and pepper	
1 lb	fusilli lunghi, linguine or spaghetti	500 g

● Scrub mussels under running water and remove any beards; discard any that do not close when tapped.

● In large saucepan, heat oil over high heat; cook onion and garlic for 2 minutes or until softened. Stir in clam juice, thyme, hot pepper sauce and tomatoes; bring to boil.

● Add mussels; cover and steam for 3 minutes. Remove mussels as they open; keep warm. Discard any that do not open.

● Cook sauce over high heat for 5 to 6 minutes or until reduced to 2-1/2 cups (625 mL). Stir in butter until melted; stir in half of the parsley. Season with salt and pepper to taste.

● Meanwhile, in large pot of boiling salted water, cook fusilli for 8 to 10 minutes or until tender but firm; drain well and toss with sauce. Arrange in center of warmed serving platter. Garnish with reserved mussels and remaining parsley. Makes 4 servings.

For an impressive platter, toss long fusilli with the sauce and surround it with mussels. If you like, remove some of the mussels from their shells while the sauce is reducing and toss them with the pasta and sauce.

Creamy Scallop Linguine with Vegetables ◀

2 tbsp	butter	25 mL
1	onion, finely chopped	1
1	clove garlic, minced	1
3 cups	thickly sliced mushrooms (12 oz/375 g)	750 mL
2	stalks celery, julienned	2
2	carrots or 1 sweet red pepper, julienned	2
2 tbsp	all-purpose flour	25 mL
3/4 cup	clam juice, fish stock or chicken stock	175 mL
1 cup	light cream	250 mL
1/2 tsp	salt	2 mL
1/4 tsp	pepper	1 mL
1 lb	scallops, halved if large	500 g
1 tsp	Pernod (optional)	5 mL
1lb	linguine	500 g

● In skillet or heavy saucepan, melt butter over medium heat; cook onion and garlic for about 3 minutes or until softened. Add mushrooms; cook, stirring occasionally, for 5 minutes. Stir in celery and carrots; cook, stirring occasionally, until tender-crisp.

● Sprinkle with flour; cook, stirring, for 1 minute. Pour in clam juice; bring to boil, stirring constantly. Whisk in cream, salt and pepper but do not boil.

● Add scallops; cook for 3 to 4 minutes or just until opaque. (Do not overcook or scallops will be tough.) Stir in Pernod (if using).

● Meanwhile, in large pot of boiling salted water, cook linguine for 8 to 10 minutes or until tender but firm; drain well. Gently toss with sauce. Makes 4 main-course or 8 appetizer servings.

Entertaining with pasta calls for a special sauce, and this creamy one, studded with scallops, suits cooking for company perfectly.

Seafood Fettuccine

1 tbsp	olive oil	15 mL
1	onion, chopped	1
2	cloves garlic, chopped	2
1 tsp	dried oregano	5 mL
Pinch	hot pepper flakes	Pinch
1	can (19 oz/540 mL) tomatoes, puréed	1
1 tsp	salt	5 mL
1/2 tsp	pepper	2 mL
1/4 cup	whipping cream	50 mL
6 oz	mussels (see sidebar, p. 32)	175 g
8 oz	deveined peeled shrimp	250 g
8 oz	scallops	250 g
12 oz	fettuccine or linguine	375 g
1/4 cup	chopped fresh parsley	50 mL

● In large saucepan, heat oil over medium heat; cook onion, garlic, oregano and hot pepper flakes, stirring, for 3 minutes or until softened.

● Stir in tomatoes, salt and pepper; bring to boil. Reduce heat and simmer for 15 to 20 minutes or until thickened. Stir in cream; simmer for 5 minutes.

● Meanwhile, scrub mussels under running water and remove any beards; discard any that do not close when tapped. Add to saucepan along with shrimp and scallops; cover and cook for 5 minutes or just until scallops are opaque, shrimp are pink and mussels have opened. Discard any mussels that do not open.

● Meanwhile, in large pot of boiling salted water, cook fettuccine until tender but firm; drain well. Toss with sauce; sprinkle with parsley. Makes 4 servings.

This special little dinner for friends also makes a gorgeous appetizer for eight.

Spaghetti with Fast Clam and Garlic Sauce

It's worth keeping a few cans of baby clams on hand to whip up this zesty dish for unexpected company.

1/4 cup	butter	50 mL
1	small onion, chopped	1
4	cloves garlic, minced	4
1/3 cup	(approx) chopped fresh parsley	75 mL
2	cans (each 5 oz/142 g) baby clams	2
1/4 cup	dry vermouth or clam juice	50 mL
1/4 tsp	each salt and pepper	1 mL
Pinch	hot pepper flakes	Pinch
12 oz	spaghetti	375 g

● In skillet, melt butter over medium heat; cook onion, garlic and parsley, stirring, for about 3 minutes or until softened.

● Drain clams, adding liquid to skillet. Add vermouth, salt, pepper and hot pepper flakes; cook for 5 to 8 minutes or until reduced by half. Add clams; cook for 1 minute.

● Meanwhile, in pot of boiling salted water, cook spaghetti for 8 to 10 minutes or until tender but firm; drain well. Toss with sauce; sprinkle with more parsley. Makes 4 servings.

Rotini with Broccoli and Clams

Purists don't serve Parmesan with seafood sauces — but with clams, the cheese does add an enjoyable finish.

1-1/3 cups	rotini	325 mL
2 cups	broccoli florets	500 mL
1 tbsp	each butter and olive oil	15 mL
2	cloves garlic, minced	2
Pinch	hot pepper flakes	Pinch
1	can (5 oz/142 g) baby clams	1
	Pepper	
1/4 cup	freshly grated Parmesan cheese	50 mL

● In large pot of boiling salted water, cook rotini for 6 minutes. Add broccoli; cook for about 2 minutes or until pasta is tender but firm. Drain well.

● Meanwhile, in large skillet, melt butter with oil over low heat; cook garlic and hot pepper flakes, stirring, for 3 minutes. Drain clams, reserving liquid. Add clams to skillet; cook until heated through. Stir in liquid.

● Add pasta mixture and increase heat to high; cook, stirring often, for about 4 minutes or until most of the liquid is absorbed. Sprinkle with pepper to taste and Parmesan. Makes 2 servings.

STOCKING THE CUPBOARD FOR PASTA

Yikes, the fridge is bare! Don't worry, though. If your cupboard is strategically stocked with the following never-be-without ingredients, you'll always be able to toss up a satisfying pasta dish in no time at all:

- tomato-based pasta sauces (include ones fortified with vegetables, mushrooms, herbs and meat)
- cans of tomatoes, tomato sauce and tomato paste
- mushrooms
- sun-dried tomatoes
- dried mushrooms
- olives
- olive oil, including extra virgin
- canned clams, tuna, salmon and anchovies
- evaporated milk
- chicken stock
- chick-peas
- onions and garlic
- dried herbs, especially basil
- hot pepper flakes
- roasted red peppers in jars
- and pasta, of course, in all your favorite shapes and sizes.

Tomato Clam Pasta ▲

1 tbsp	olive oil	15 mL
1	large onion, chopped	1
3	cloves garlic, minced	3
1	can (28 oz/796 mL) stewed tomatoes	1
3 tbsp	tomato paste	50 mL
1	can (5 oz/142 g) baby clams	1
1/2 tsp	dried oregano	2 mL
Pinch	hot pepper flakes	Pinch
1 tsp	dried parsley	5 mL
	Salt and pepper	
4 cups	rotini	1 L
1/2 cup	freshly grated Parmesan cheese	125 mL

● In heavy saucepan, heat oil over medium heat; cook onion and garlic, stirring, for about 5 minutes or until softened. Add tomatoes, crushing with fork; stir in tomato paste.

● Drain clams, pouring juice into saucepan; set clams aside. Stir in oregano and hot pepper flakes; bring to boil. Reduce heat and simmer for 30 minutes or until thickened. Add clams, parsley, and salt and pepper to taste; heat through.

● Meanwhile, in large pot of boiling salted water, cook rotini for 6 to 8 minutes or until tender but firm; drain well. Toss with sauce; sprinkle with Parmesan. Makes 4 servings.

F*or extra color, add zucchini and carrots to the onions while they cook.*

Spinach Fettuccine with Cauliflower and Anchovy Sauce ▲

The rich flavors of olive oil, garlic and anchovies blend subtly with cauliflower and Parmesan cheese to make a delightful, almost creamy, sauce.

12 oz	spinach fettuccine	375 g
4 cups	cauliflower florets (about half a head)	1 L
3 tbsp	extra virgin olive oil	50 mL
1	clove garlic, minced	1
4	anchovy fillets, minced (or 2 tsp/10 mL anchovy paste)	4
2 tbsp	butter	25 mL
1/3 cup	freshly grated Parmesan cheese	75 mL
	Pepper	

● In large pot of boiling salted water, cook fettuccine for 8 to 10 minutes or until tender but firm; drain well.

● Meanwhile, steam cauliflower for about 3 minutes or until tender-crisp.

● In large skillet, heat oil over medium heat; cook garlic for 1 minute. Add anchovies; cook, stirring, for 2 minutes.

● Toss cauliflower, anchovies and butter with fettuccine. Add Parmesan, and pepper to taste; toss again. Makes 4 servings.

Penne with Anchovy Tomato Sauce

1 tbsp	olive oil	15 mL
3	cloves garlic, minced	3
1/4 tsp	hot pepper flakes	1 mL
3	anchovies, chopped	3
1	can (28 oz/796 mL) tomatoes, drained	1
1/4 cup	chopped fresh parsley	50 mL
1/4 tsp	each salt and pepper	1 mL
5 cups	penne or fusilli	1.25 L

● In skillet, heat oil over low heat; cook garlic and hot pepper flakes for 3 minutes or until garlic is softened but not browned. Add anchovies; cook for 1 minute.

● Increase heat to medium-high. Add tomatoes, breaking up with spoon; cook, stirring occasionally, for 5 minutes or until thickened slightly. Stir in parsley, salt and pepper.

● Meanwhile, in large pot of boiling salted water, cook penne for 8 to 10 minutes or until tender but firm; drain well. Toss with sauce. Makes 4 servings.

If you're the kind of person who always says, "Hold the anchovies," this recipe may make you change your mind! Once cooked, there is only the mellowest hint of them in the flavorful sauce.

Spaghetti with Anchovies, Walnuts and Garlic

2	cans (50 g each) anchovy fillets (packed in oil)	2
1/2 cup	extra virgin olive oil	125 mL
8	cloves garlic, minced	8
12 oz	spaghetti or vermicelli	375 g
1/2 cup	walnuts, finely chopped	125 mL
1/3 cup	chopped fresh parsley	75 mL

● Drain anchovies; rinse under cold water. Pat dry and chop.

● In large skillet, heat oil over low heat; cook garlic and anchovies, stirring occasionally, for about 15 minutes or until garlic is lightly golden.

● Meanwhile, in large pot of boiling salted water, cook spaghetti for 8 to 10 minutes or until tender but firm; drain well. Toss with sauce, walnuts and parsley. Makes 4 servings.

Anchovies full steam ahead with garlic and a simple toss of spaghetti. This unusual little sauce is just right for a small dinner party starter.

Linguine with Salmon and Dill

1 cup	ricotta cheese	250 mL
3/4 cup	milk	175 mL
2 tbsp	butter	25 mL
1	clove garlic, minced	1
4	green onions, finely chopped	4
1 tbsp	chopped fresh dill (or 1 tsp/5 mL dried dillweed)	15 mL
6 oz	smoked salmon, cut into strips	175 g
12 oz	linguine or spaghetti	375 g
1/2 tsp	pepper	2 mL
1/4 cup	freshly grated Parmesan cheese (optional)	50 mL

● In food processor or blender, purée together ricotta and milk until smooth; set aside.

● In skillet, melt butter over medium heat; cook garlic, onions and dill, stirring, for about 3 minutes or until softened. Add salmon and ricotta mixture; cook over low heat for about 3 minutes or until heated through.

● Meanwhile, in large pot of boiling salted water, cook linguine for 8 to 10 minutes or until tender but firm; drain well. Toss with sauce; sprinkle with pepper, and Parmesan (if using). Makes 4 servings.

All you need is a little smoked salmon to flavor this delightful pasta dish. The surprise is that it's not cream that gives the sauce its wonderful texture — it's a puréed blend of milk and ricotta cheese.

Wok, Pot and Skillet

From trendy stir-fried Pad Thai to easy frittata in a skillet or minestrone by the bowl, pasta is the versatile star of all these dishes — and more!

Minestrone Warm-Up ▶

You don't have to speak Italian to know that "minestrone" translates into a nourishing bean and pasta soup chock-full of flavor and satisfaction.

1 cup	dried red or white kidney beans	250 mL
1 tbsp	olive oil	15 mL
4 oz	pancetta or bacon (unsliced), cubed	125 g
2	cloves garlic, minced	2
2	onions, chopped	2
8 cups	chicken stock	2 L
2	each carrots and stalks celery, diagonally sliced	2
Half	small cabbage, shredded	Half
1	can (28 oz/796 mL) tomatoes, mashed	1
1	bay leaf	1
1 tsp	each dried basil and oregano	5 mL
1/2 tsp	salt	2 mL
1/4 tsp	pepper	1 mL
3	potatoes, peeled and cubed	3
1 cup	rotini, macaroni or tubetti	250 mL
	PARSLEY PESTO	
1 cup	packed fresh parsley	250 mL
1/4 cup	extra virgin olive oil	50 mL
2 tbsp	pine nuts or walnuts	25 mL
1	clove garlic, minced	1
1/4 cup	freshly grated Parmesan cheese	50 mL
	Salt and pepper	

● In bowl, cover beans with 3 cups (750 mL) water. Cover and soak overnight; drain, discarding water.

● In Dutch oven, heat oil over medium-high heat; cook pancetta, garlic and onions for 5 minutes or until softened.

● Add beans and stock; bring to boil, skimming off foam. Cover and simmer over medium-low heat for 1 hour or until beans are tender.

● Add carrots, celery, cabbage, tomatoes, bay leaf, basil, oregano, salt and pepper; bring to boil. Reduce heat, cover and simmer for 20 minutes. Add potatoes and rotini; simmer, covered, for 10 to 15 minutes or until potatoes are tender. Discard bay leaf.

● PARSLEY PESTO: Meanwhile, in food processor, purée parsley, oil and pine nuts until smooth; transfer to bowl. Stir in garlic and Parmesan. Season with salt and pepper to taste.

● Ladle soup into bowls; top each with 1 tbsp (15 mL) pesto. Makes 8 servings.

TIP: You can make the soup ahead of time and refrigerate it for up to 5 days. To freeze it for up to 1 month, omit the potatoes and pasta. Add them when reheating by simmering, covered, for 10 to 15 minutes or until potatoes are tender, adding more chicken stock if desired.

Speedy Tomato, Chick-Pea and Spinach Soup ▶

January cold holds no threat when you come home to this chunky soup. Grate or shave a little cheese over the top and serve with whole grain bread or focaccia.

2 cups	vegetable stock	500 mL
1	can (28 oz/796 mL) tomatoes	1
1	onion, chopped	1
1	clove garlic, minced	1
1/4 tsp	dried sage	1 mL
1 cup	rotini	250 mL
1	can (19 oz/540 mL) chick-peas, drained and rinsed	1
2 cups	chopped fresh spinach	500 mL
1/4 tsp	pepper	1 mL
Dash	hot pepper sauce	Dash

● In large saucepan, combine stock and tomatoes, breaking up with fork. Add onion, garlic and sage; bring to boil. Add rotini and reduce heat to medium-low; cover and simmer for 7 minutes.

● Add chick-peas and spinach; cover and cook for 3 minutes or until pasta is tender but firm. Stir in pepper and hot pepper sauce. Makes 4 to 6 servings.

Starry Stracciatella

This chicken-broth-and-swirled-egg soup spells instant supper. The pasta stars (stellini) and peas add substance.

2	cans (each 10 oz/284 mL) chicken broth	2
1/2 cup	stellini	125 mL
1 cup	frozen peas	250 mL
1	egg	1
1/3 cup	freshly grated Parmesan cheese	75 mL

● In saucepan, bring broth and 3-1/2 cups (875 mL) water to boil. Stir in stellini; cook for 3 minutes. Add peas; cook for 2 minutes or until pasta is tender but firm.

● In bowl and using fork, beat egg; gradually pour into broth mixture, stirring with fork to keep mixture stringy. Serve sprinkled with Parmesan. Makes 6 servings.

Oriental Shrimp Noodle Soup ▶

For extra flavor, add a splash of sherry to the soup just before serving.

2 tsp	vegetable oil	10 mL
1	onion, chopped	1
2	cloves garlic, minced	2
1 tbsp	minced gingerroot	15 mL
Pinch	hot pepper flakes (optional)	Pinch
8 cups	chicken stock	2 L
1 cup	each diagonally sliced carrot and celery	250 mL
2 cups	snow peas, halved	500 mL
12 oz	shrimp, peeled and deveined	375 g
4 oz	rice vermicelli	125 g
2 tbsp	soy sauce	25 mL
1/4 tsp	pepper	1 mL

● In Dutch oven or large saucepan, heat oil over medium heat; cook onion, garlic, ginger, and hot pepper flakes (if using) for 3 minutes or until softened.

● Add stock, carrot and celery; bring to boil. Reduce heat to medium-low; cover and simmer for 5 minutes. Add snow peas and shrimp; simmer, covered, for 3 minutes.

● Break vermicelli into 2-inch (5 cm) pieces and add to soup; cover and simmer for 2 to 3 minutes or until vegetables are tender and shrimp are pink. Stir in soy sauce and pepper. Makes 5 to 7 servings.

Cheesy Pasta Frittata ▼

This easy meal-in-a-skillet is one the whole family will enjoy. In season, take advantage of fresh peas and corn. Any short pasta, such as penne or macaroni, can be used.

1 cup	fusilli	250 mL
1 tbsp	butter	15 mL
1 tbsp	olive oil	15 mL
1	onion, chopped	1
1/2 cup	sliced mushrooms	125 mL
1/2 cup	corn kernels	125 mL
1/2 cup	peas	125 mL
8	eggs	8
1/2 cup	shredded Cheddar cheese	125 mL
1/2 tsp	salt	2 mL
1/4 tsp	pepper	1 mL
	SALSA	
2 cups	chopped seeded tomatoes	500 mL

1 tbsp	chopped fresh basil	15 mL
1 tsp	olive oil	5 mL
1	clove garlic, minced	1
Dash	hot pepper sauce	Dash
	Salt and pepper	

● In large pot of boiling salted water, cook fusilli for 8 to 10 minutes or until tender but firm; drain well.

● Salsa: Meanwhile, combine tomatoes, basil, oil, garlic, hot pepper sauce, and salt and pepper to taste; set aside.

● In 9-inch (23 cm) ovenproof skillet, heat butter and oil over medium heat; cook onion and mushrooms for 3 minutes or until tender. Add fusilli, corn and peas; toss to mix well.

● Whisk together eggs, cheese, salt and pepper; pour into skillet.

● Cook for 5 to 8 minutes or until bottom is set. Bake in 350°F (180°C) oven for 5 to 7 minutes or until slightly puffy and set in center but still moist. Cut frittata into wedges; serve with salsa. Makes 6 servings.

Spaghetti Frittata

8 oz	spaghetti	250 g
1/3 cup	freshly grated Parmesan cheese	75 mL
1/4 cup	butter	50 mL
2 tbsp	chopped fresh parsley	25 mL
4	eggs	4
1/2 tsp	each salt and pepper	2 mL

● In large pot of boiling salted water, cook spaghetti for 8 to 10 minutes or until tender but firm; drain well. Transfer to bowl. Stir in cheese, 3 tbsp (50 mL) of the butter and parsley; let cool slightly.

● Beat together eggs, salt and pepper; add to spaghetti mixture, mixing well.

● In large nonstick skillet, heat remaining butter over medium heat until foaming; pour in spaghetti mixture and spread evenly. Cook for 4 to 5 minutes or until bottom is golden brown.

● Loosen frittata with spatula; invert onto plate. Slide frittata back into skillet and cook for 3 to 4 minutes or until bottom is golden brown. Cut into wedges to serve. Makes 4 servings.

This Italian-style omelette makes a quick low-cost dinner and is a great way to use up leftover pasta.

Mexican-Style Pork Chop and Spaghetti Bake

3 tbsp	vegetable oil	50 mL
1	onion, chopped	1
2	cloves garlic, minced	2
1	can (19 oz/540 mL) tomatoes	1
1	can (114 mL) diced green chilies, drained and rinsed	1
1 tbsp	chopped fresh parsley	15 mL
2 tsp	chili powder	10 mL
1 tsp	ground cumin	5 mL
1/2 tsp	dried oregano	2 mL
4 cups	boiling water	1 L
8 oz	spaghetti, broken in half	250 g
4	pork chops	4
Pinch	each salt and pepper	Pinch
3/4 cup	shredded Cheddar cheese	175 mL
	Parsley sprigs	

● In large saucepan, heat 2 tbsp (25 mL) of the oil over medium heat; cook onion and garlic for 3 minutes or until softened.

● Add tomatoes, breaking up with fork. Stir in green chilies, parsley, chili powder, cumin and oregano. Stir in boiling water and bring to boil; add spaghetti. Reduce heat to medium-low; cover and simmer, stirring occasionally, for 20 to 25 minutes or until most of the liquid has been absorbed.

● Meanwhile, trim fat from chops. In large ovenproof skillet, heat remaining oil over medium-high heat; cook chops, without turning, for 10 minutes. Turn chops over and sprinkle with salt and pepper; cover and cook for 5 minutes longer or just until no longer pink inside but still moist.

● Remove chops from skillet and drain off any fat. Spread spaghetti mixture in skillet; top with chops. *(Recipe can be prepared to this point, cooled, covered and refrigerated for up to 6 hours. Heat in 350°F/180°C oven for 20 minutes before continuing.)*

● Sprinkle cheese over chops; bake in 350°F (180°C) oven for 5 to 10 minutes or until cheese melts. Garnish with parsley. Makes 4 servings.

This easy pork chop and pasta skillet supper is perfect any day of the week. Serve it right away or make it ahead of time for a satisfying no-fuss meal in minutes.

Pad Thai ◄

1	pkg (227 g) wide rice stick noodles	1
1/2 cup	chicken stock	125 mL
1/4 cup	granulated sugar	50 mL
1/4 cup	fish sauce	50 mL
3 tbsp	lime juice	45 mL
2 tbsp	ketchup	25 mL
1/4 tsp	hot pepper flakes	1 mL
4 oz	boneless pork loin	125 g
6 oz	firm tofu	175 g
1/4 cup	vegetable oil	50 mL
1	egg, beaten	1
3	cloves garlic, minced	3
8 oz	large raw shrimp, peeled and deveined	250 g
1	sweet red pepper, diced	1
2 cups	bean sprouts	500 mL
1/2 cup	coriander leaves, coarsely chopped	125 mL
6	green onions, thinly sliced	6
1/4 cup	unsalted peanuts, chopped	50 mL

● In large bowl, soak noodles in warm water for 15 minutes; drain and set aside.

● Meanwhile, in small bowl, whisk together chicken stock, sugar, fish sauce, lime juice, ketchup and hot pepper flakes; set sauce aside.

● Cut pork across the grain into 1/4-inch (5 mm) thick strips. Cut tofu into 1/2-inch (1 cm) cubes. Set aside.

● In wok or large skillet, heat 1 tsp (5 mL) of the oil over medium heat; cook egg, stirring occasionally, for about 3 minutes or until scrambled and set. Transfer to large plate.

● Wipe out wok; add 1 tbsp (15 mL) of the oil. Increase heat to medium-high; stir-fry garlic, shrimp and pork for about 3 minutes or until shrimp are bright pink. Add to egg.

● Heat remaining oil in pan. Stir in tofu and red pepper; cook, stirring occasionally, for 2 minutes or until tofu begins to brown. Gently stir in noodles for 1 minute or until beginning to wilt. Pour in sauce; stir-fry for 3 minutes or until noodles are tender.

● Return egg mixture to pan; add bean sprouts, coriander and half of the green onions. Stir-fry for 2 to 3 minutes or until heated through. Remove to warmed serving platter; garnish with peanuts and remaining green onions. Makes 4 servings.

This supper-size stir-fried noodle salad from Thailand is a symphony of flavors and textures. The lilt of fresh coriander and lime plays along with assertive garlic, sweet shrimp, salty fish sauce and crunchy bean sprouts.

TIPS:

● Soaking times for rice noodles are important because the noodles absorb liquid as long as they are in it and can become too soft and swollen.

● For a change of taste, substitute a 4 oz (125 g) boneless skinless chicken breast for the pork. If rice noodles are unavailable, 12 oz (375 g) fettuccine, cooked, can be stirred into the wok after the tofu.

THAI INGREDIENTS

Coriander, often known by its Spanish translation, cilantro, is the soul of Thai food, here adding a punch of its aromatic funky flavor right at the very end.
Fish Sauce is a clear amber-colored sauce, either shrimp- or anchovy-flavored, used extensively in Southeast Asian cooking to provide saltiness and to enhance the taste of other ingredients. Store opened bottle in refrigerator.

Skillet Turkey and Pasta Supper

When there's not much time, this satisfying one-pot supper is sure to please. Made with turkey and no added fat, it's a lean and tasty update of the old hamburger pasta supper.

12 oz	ground turkey	375 g
1	onion, chopped	1
1	sweet green pepper, chopped	1
1	clove garlic, minced	1
1/2 tsp	each dried thyme and salt	2 mL
1/4 tsp	pepper	1 mL
1	can (28 oz/796 mL) stewed tomatoes	1
2 tbsp	tomato paste	25 mL
1-1/2 cups	rotini	375 mL

● In large nonstick skillet, cook turkey over high heat, stirring often, for 3 to 5 minutes or until no longer pink. Drain off any fat.

● Add onion, green pepper, garlic, thyme, salt and pepper; cook, stirring, for 3 minutes. Add tomatoes, breaking up with spoon. Add tomato paste and 1/2 cup (125 mL) water; bring to boil.

● Add rotini and reduce heat to low; partially cover and cook, stirring often, for 20 to 25 minutes or until thickened and pasta is tender but firm. Makes 4 servings.

Sesame Tofu and Vegetable Stir-Fry ▶

Tofu is the chameleon of cooking, taking on the flavors of companion ingredients. In this one-dish supper, the flavor it drinks up is the classic Oriental soy sauce and sesame oil combination.

2 cups	broken rice vermicelli	500 mL
8 oz	tofu	250 g
1/4 cup	soy sauce	50 mL
2 tbsp	sherry or Marsala wine	25 mL
1	clove garlic, minced	1
6	green onions	6
2 tbsp	butter	25 mL
1 tbsp	sesame oil	15 mL
1-1/2 cups	small broccoli florets	375 mL
1 cup	thinly sliced carrot	250 mL
10	mushrooms, thickly sliced	10
1 tbsp	slivered gingerroot	15 mL
2 tbsp	toasted sesame seeds	25 mL

● In large bowl, pour boiling water over vermicelli; let stand for 15 minutes. Drain well and set aside.

● Cut tofu into 3/4-inch (2 cm) thick slices; arrange in single layer in small dish. Combine soy sauce, sherry and garlic; pour over tofu and marinate for 10 minutes.

● Reserving 2 tbsp (25 mL) marinade, transfer slices to plate lined with double thickness of paper towels; cover with double thickness of paper towels. Place plate on top and weigh down with heavy cans; let stand for 3 minutes. Cut into 1/2-inch (1 cm) pieces. Set aside.

● Cut green onions diagonally into thin slices; set green and white parts aside separately.

● In skillet, heat butter with oil over medium heat; stir-fry white part of onions for 1 minute. Add broccoli and carrot; stir-fry for 4 minutes.

● Add mushrooms and ginger; stir-fry for 2 minutes. Add green part of onions and tofu; stir-fry for 2 minutes. Add vermicelli, reserved marinade and sesame seeds; toss gently and heat through. Makes 4 servings.

TIP: Pressing tofu before cooking with it helps keep it from crumbling. Look for firm or extra-firm tofu for this dish.

Great Bakes

Under crispy golden toppings lie layers of deliciously melted cheese, tender pasta and a variety of vegetables, meats and seafood guaranteed to comfort and please.

Easy Lasagna ▶

Satisfying lasagna is a guaranteed crowd-pleaser at any potluck or buffet. Here's an easy-to-make version that delivers all the great taste with a minimum of work. Best of all, it can be made up to 1 day ahead.

8 oz	lasagna noodles	250 g
1	pkg (300 g) frozen chopped spinach, thawed and squeezed dry	1
2 cups	shredded mozzarella cheese	500 mL
1/4 cup	freshly grated Parmesan cheese	50 mL
	MEAT FILLING	
8 oz	Italian sausage	250 g
8 oz	ground beef	250 g
1	each onion, carrot and stalk celery, chopped	1
4	cloves garlic, minced	4
1-1/2 tsp	each dried oregano and basil	7 mL
Pinch	hot pepper flakes	Pinch
1	can (28 oz/796 mL) tomatoes	1
1	can (14 oz/398 mL) tomato sauce	1
1/4 tsp	pepper	1 mL
	CHEESE FILLING	
2	eggs	2
1/4 tsp	each pepper and nutmeg	1 mL
2 cups	cottage cheese	500 mL
1 cup	shredded mozzarella cheese	250 mL
1/2 cup	freshly grated Parmesan cheese	125 mL

● MEAT FILLING: Remove sausage from casing; crumble meat. In Dutch oven, cook sausage and beef over medium-high heat, breaking up with spoon, for about 5 minutes or until no longer pink; remove to plate. Spoon off all but 1 tbsp (15 mL) fat from pot.

● Add onion, carrot, celery, garlic, oregano, basil and hot pepper flakes; cook, stirring, for 3 to 5 minutes or until softened. Add tomatoes, tomato sauce and meat; bring to boil. Reduce heat and simmer, breaking up tomatoes and stirring often, for 20 to 25 minutes or until thickened. Add pepper.

● CHEESE FILLING: In bowl, whisk together eggs, pepper and nutmeg. Blend in cottage cheese, mozzarella and Parmesan.

● Meanwhile, in large pot of boiling salted water, cook noodles for 6 to 8 minutes or until almost tender. Drain and cool in cold water. Remove and arrange in single layer on damp tea towel.

● Spread 1 cup (250 mL) of the meat filling as base in greased 13- x 9-inch (3 L) baking dish. Top with one-third of the noodles in single layer; spread with one-third of the remaining meat filling. Spread with half of the cheese filling, then half of the spinach. Starting with noodles, repeat layers once.

● Top with remaining noodles; spread with remaining meat filling. Sprinkle with mozzarella and Parmesan. Cover loosely with foil.

● Bake in 375°F (190°C) oven for 20 minutes. Uncover and bake for 20 to 25 minutes longer or until bubbling and heated through. Let stand for 10 minutes before serving. Makes 8 servings.

Seafood and Spinach Lasagna

Lobster and shrimp transform lasagna into special-occasion company fare. For good value, look to Atlantic frozen-pack shelled lobster — it's all meat. When mixed with shrimp and monkfish or sole, it feeds a group generously and stylishly.

12 oz	spinach lasagna noodles	375 g
	SEAFOOD LAYER	
1	onion, minced	1
1 cup	dry white wine or fish stock	250 mL
1 lb	monkfish or sole	500 g
1	can (11.3 oz/320 g) frozen lobster meat, thawed and drained	1
8 oz	small cooked shrimp	250 g
	SPINACH SAUCE	
1/4 cup	butter	50 mL
1/4 cup	all-purpose flour	50 mL
3 cups	milk	750 mL
3 cups	shredded mozzarella cheese	750 mL
3/4 cup	freshly grated Parmesan cheese	175 mL
1	pkg (10 oz/284 g) fresh spinach, cooked and squeezed dry	1
1-1/2 tsp	salt	7 mL
1/2 tsp	each nutmeg and hot pepper sauce	2 mL

● SEAFOOD LAYER: In saucepan, bring onion and wine to simmer over low heat; cover and simmer for 5 minutes. Cut fish into 1/2-inch (1 cm) pieces; add to pan and simmer, covered, for 5 minutes. Pour into sieve set over large measure, reserving 1 cup (250 mL) liquid. Chop lobster into bite-size pieces; combine with fish mixture and shrimp.

● SPINACH SAUCE: In heavy saucepan, melt butter over medium heat; stir in flour and cook, whisking, for 2 minutes, without browning. Whisk in reserved fish-poaching liquid and milk; bring to boil. Reduce heat and simmer, whisking occasionally, for 5 minutes or until thickened and smooth; remove from heat. Stir in half of the mozzarella and Parmesan, the spinach, salt, nutmeg and hot pepper sauce.

● Meanwhile, in large pot of boiling salted water, cook noodles for 6 to 8 minutes or until almost tender. Drain and cool in cold water; remove and arrange in single layer on damp tea towel.

● Arrange 3 noodles in single layer in well-greased 13- x 9-inch (3 L) baking dish. Spread with one-quarter of the sauce and one-third of the seafood. Repeat layers twice. Top with remaining noodles, then sauce. Sprinkle with remaining mozzarella and Parmesan. *(Lasagna can be prepared to this point, covered and refrigerated for up to 8 hours. Add 10 minutes to baking time.)*

● Bake in 325°F (160°C) oven for 45 to 60 minutes or until golden brown and bubbling. Let stand for 10 minutes before serving. Makes 12 servings.

COOKING SPINACH

● To cook fresh spinach, first rinse thoroughly in several changes of water, allowing sand to fall to bottom of sink. Slightly warm water relaxes crinkly leaves and releases more grit.

● Shake off excess water and transfer spinach to large heavy saucepan; cover and cook, with just the water clinging to leaves, over medium-high heat for about 5 minutes or until spinach has just wilted.

● Remove from heat and drain in sieve, pressing out moisture if spinach is destined for a stuffing or baked pasta layer.

● Frozen spinach can replace the fresh cooked spinach as a time-saver. Just let it thaw, press out excess moisture and follow instructions for cooked spinach.

Lightened-Up Lasagna

1 tbsp	olive oil	15 mL
1	onion, chopped	1
3	green onions, chopped	3
2	cloves garlic, minced	2
1/4 tsp	hot pepper flakes	1 mL
1 lb	ground chicken	500 g
1-1/2 cups	finely chopped sweet red pepper	375 mL
1 cup	each finely chopped carrots and celery	250 mL
2	cans (each 28 oz/796 mL) tomatoes, puréed	2
1 tsp	(approx) salt	5 mL
1/2 tsp	(approx) pepper	2 mL
1/4 cup	chopped fresh parsley	50 mL
2 cups	low-fat cottage cheese	500 mL
12 oz	lasagna noodles	375 g
2 cups	shredded low-fat mozzarella cheese (about 8 oz/250 g)	500 mL

● In Dutch oven, heat oil over medium heat; cook onion, green onions, garlic and hot pepper flakes for about 5 minutes or until softened. Add chicken; cook, stirring, for 5 minutes or until no longer pink.

● Add red pepper, carrots and celery; cook, stirring, for 5 minutes. Add tomatoes and bring to boil; add salt and pepper. Reduce heat to medium-low; simmer gently for 35 to 45 minutes or until thickened. Stir in parsley. Season cottage cheese with salt and pepper to taste.

● Meanwhile, in large pot of boiling salted water, cook noodles for 6 to 8 minutes or until almost tender. Drain and cool in cold water. Remove and arrange in single layer on damp tea towel.

● Arrange one-quarter of the noodles in single layer in greased 13- x 9-inch (3 L) baking dish. Spread with half of the cottage cheese and one-quarter of the sauce; sprinkle with one-quarter of the mozzarella. Repeat layer of noodles, sauce and mozzarella.

● Repeat layer of noodles, cottage cheese, sauce and mozzarella; top with layer of noodles, sauce and mozzarella. Cover with foil and bake in 375°F (190°C) oven for 50 minutes; uncover and bake for 10 minutes longer or until golden and bubbling. Let stand for 10 minutes before serving. Makes 8 servings.

Reduced oil and low-fat ground chicken, cottage cheese and mozzarella make this lasagna lighter than most, and just as tasty.

Conchiglie with Zucchini and Spinach ◄

1	box (12 oz/375 g) jumbo conchiglie	1
1 cup	freshly grated Parmesan cheese	250 mL
	FILLING	
3	medium zucchini	3
	Salt	
1	bunch spinach (about 8 oz/250 g)	1
1/4 cup	butter	50 mL
2	onions, finely chopped	2
1	clove garlic, minced	1
1 lb	ricotta cheese	500 g
1 cup	freshly grated Parmesan cheese	250 mL
2	eggs	2
1/4 cup	chopped fresh basil or parsley	50 mL
1/4 tsp	each pepper and nutmeg	1 mL
	SAUCE	
1/4 cup	butter	50 mL
2	onions, finely chopped	2
2	cloves garlic, minced	2
2	cans (each 28 oz/796 mL) tomatoes	2
	Salt and pepper	

● FILLING: Grate zucchini and place in colander. Sprinkle with 2 tsp (10 mL) salt; let drain for 30 minutes. Rinse and drain well; drain on paper towels.

● Trim spinach and rinse under water; shake off excess water. In saucepan, cover spinach and cook, with just the water clinging to leaves, over medium-high heat for about 5 minutes or just until wilted. Drain well and squeeze dry; chop coarsely and set aside.

● In large heavy skillet, melt butter over medium heat; cook onions and garlic for about 5 minutes or until tender. Add zucchini; cook until any moisture has evaporated. Add spinach and mix well. Let cool; drain off excess liquid.

● In large bowl, beat ricotta until smooth; beat in Parmesan, eggs, basil, 1 tsp (5 mL) salt, pepper and nutmeg. Stir in zucchini mixture until combined; set aside.

● SAUCE: In saucepan, melt butter over medium heat; cook onions and garlic for about 5 minutes or until softened. Add tomatoes, breaking up with spoon; cook for 30 to 45 minutes or until thickened. Purée in food processor; season with salt and pepper to taste. Set aside.

● In large pot of boiling salted water, cook conchiglie for 8 to 10 minutes or until tender but firm; drain and refresh under cold water. Gently shake conchiglie in colander to drain excess water. Coarsely chop any broken conchiglie; place in greased 13- x 9-inch (3 L) baking dish.

● Spoon some of the filling into each conchiglie; arrange, stuffed side up, over chopped ones. Pour sauce over top; sprinkle with Parmesan. Bake in 350°F (180° C) oven for 40 to 50 minutes or until bubbling. Makes 8 servings.

TIP: Jumbo pasta shells are easier to work with and fill than the tiny ones. If you can find only small shells, don't try to fill them. Simply layer them with the filling and sauce.

J*umbo pasta shells (conchiglie), stuffed with a cheesy spinach and zucchini filling and napped with a robust tomato sauce, are more than worth the effort. This hearty vegetarian pasta dish is an excellent addition to any potluck supper.*

Tuna Florentine ▼

Spinach, which provides the Florentine touch, is a natural with pasta. Keep this easy dish in mind for weeknight suppers, and make it even easier by replacing the fresh spinach with a package of frozen.

2 tbsp	butter	25 mL
1	onion, sliced	1
1	clove garlic, minced	1
1	can (19 oz/540 mL) tomatoes	1
1	can (7-1/2 oz/213 mL) tomato sauce	1
1/2 tsp	each dried basil, granulated sugar and salt	2 mL
1/4 tsp	pepper	1 mL
4 oz	medium egg noodles	125 g
1	pkg (10 oz/284 g) fresh spinach	1
1	can (6-1/2 oz/184 g) tuna, drained	1
1/4 cup	freshly grated Parmesan cheese	50 mL

● In large skillet, melt butter over medium heat; cook onion and garlic for about 3 minutes or until softened. Stir in tomatoes, tomato sauce, basil, sugar, salt and pepper; simmer for about 20 minutes or until thickened.

● Meanwhile, in large pot of boiling salted water, cook noodles for 8 to 10 minutes or until tender but firm; drain well and set aside.

● Rinse spinach; shake off excess water. In saucepan, cover spinach and cook, with just the water clinging to leaves, over medium-high heat for about 5 minutes or just until wilted. Drain well and squeeze dry; chop coarsely and set aside.

● Break tuna into chunks and stir into tomato mixture along with cooked noodles. Transfer to 6-cup (1.5 L) casserole. Spoon chopped spinach around edge. Sprinkle Parmesan over top. Bake in 375°F (190°C) oven for about 25 minutes or until bubbling. Makes 4 to 6 servings.

Nouvelle Tuna Casserole

2	pkg (each 10 oz/284 g) fresh spinach, trimmed	2
1/3 cup	butter	75 mL
3	onions, chopped	3
1/2 cup	all-purpose flour	125 mL
6 cups	milk	1.5 L
2 tsp	each dried basil and salt	10 mL
1 tsp	pepper	5 mL
Pinch	hot pepper flakes	Pinch
4 cups	fusilli or penne	1 L
3	cans (each 7-1/2 oz/213 g) tuna, drained and broken into chunks	3
2 cups	shredded old Cheddar cheese	500 mL
2 tbsp	lemon juice	25 mL
	TOPPING	
3 cups	fresh bread crumbs	750 mL
1 cup	shredded old Cheddar cheese	250 mL
1 tbsp	butter, melted	15 mL
1 tbsp	Dijon mustard	15 mL

● Rinse spinach; shake off excess water. In stockpot, cover spinach and cook, with just the water clinging to leaves, over medium-high heat for about 5 minutes or just until wilted. Drain well and squeeze dry; chop coarsely and set aside.

● In large saucepan, melt butter over medium heat; cook onions for 3 minutes or until softened. Stir in flour; cook, whisking, for 3 minutes, without browning. Gradually whisk in milk until smooth; cook, whisking often, for about 15 minutes or until boiling and thickened. Reduce heat to low. Season with basil, salt, pepper and hot pepper flakes.

● Meanwhile, in large pot of boiling salted water, cook fusilli for 8 to 10 minutes or until tender but firm. Drain and refresh under cold water; drain again and return to pot. Add sauce, spinach, tuna, Cheddar and lemon juice; toss to combine. Divide between two greased 8-inch (2 L) square baking dishes, spreading evenly.

● TOPPING: Toss together bread crumbs, Cheddar, butter and mustard; sprinkle over casseroles. Cover loosely with foil. *(Casseroles can be prepared to this point, covered and refrigerated for up to 1 day or wrapped well and frozen for up to 2 months. Thaw completely in refrigerator. Bake for 25 to 30 minutes longer than specified, uncovering for last 10 minutes.)*

● Bake in 350°F (180°C) oven for 20 minutes; uncover and bake for 25 minutes longer or until heated through and golden. Makes 8 servings.

Fresh spinach, old Cheddar, fusilli and basil update a family favorite. Since the recipe makes enough for two 8-inch (2 L) square baking dishes, enjoy one casserole right away and store the second in the freezer for up to 2 months.

Comfy Macaroni and Cheese

2 cups	macaroni	500 mL
2 cups	shredded mozzarella cheese	500 mL
1-1/2 cups	sour cream	375 mL
1 cup	diced ham	250 mL
1 cup	cottage cheese	250 mL
1/2 cup	chopped sweet red pepper	125 mL
1	egg, lightly beaten	1
1/4 tsp	each salt and pepper	1 mL

● In large pot of boiling salted water, cook macaroni for 8 to 10 minutes or until tender but firm; drain well.

● In large bowl, combine 1-1/2 cups (375 mL) of the mozzarella, sour cream, ham, cottage cheese, red pepper, egg, salt and pepper. Add macaroni and mix well.

● Pour into greased 8-inch (2 L) square baking dish; sprinkle with remaining mozzarella. Bake in 350°F (180°C) oven for 30 minutes or until bubbling. Broil for 2 minutes or until lightly golden. Makes 4 servings.

For most of us, macaroni was our introduction to pasta — cheese-rich and fork-tender under a crunchy topping. Here's an update with trendy peppers, a bit of ham and lots of creaminess from cottage cheese, mozzarella and sour cream.

Macaroni Tomato Pie

This colorful variation on macaroni and cheese makes a quick and tasty supper any day of the week.

1-1/4 cups	macaroni	300 mL
1	egg, beaten	1
1-1/2 cups	shredded Cheddar cheese	375 mL
1	can (19 oz/540 mL) stewed tomatoes	1
1/4 tsp	each salt, pepper, dried oregano and basil	1 mL
1 cup	fresh bread crumbs	250 mL
1 tbsp	butter, melted	15 mL

● In large pot of boiling salted water, cook macaroni for 8 to 10 minutes or until tender but firm; drain well.

● Stir in egg and 1 cup (250 mL) of the Cheddar. Spread over bottom and side of greased 9-inch (23 cm) pie plate.

● Stir together tomatoes, salt, pepper, oregano and basil; pour into macaroni shell. Sprinkle with remaining Cheddar.

● Toss bread crumbs with butter; sprinkle over top, covering edge of macaroni shell. Bake in 350°F (180°C) oven for 25 to 30 minutes or until golden. Makes 4 servings.

Cheesy Wild Mushroom Casserole

It takes only a tiny package of wild mushrooms to boost the flavor of a whole panful of pasta. Choose dried porcini or morels, and add a bounty of fresh mushrooms.

7 cups	rigatoni	1.75 L
1 cup	shredded Fontina or Swiss cheese	250 mL
4 oz	Gorgonzola or mild blue cheese, crumbled	125 g
1-1/2 cups	freshly grated Parmesan cheese	375 mL
	MUSHROOM LAYER	
1-1/2 cups	warm water	375 mL
1	pkg (1/2 oz/15 g) dried wild mushrooms	1
1/4 cup	butter	50 mL
3	onions, finely chopped	3
6 cups	sliced fresh mushrooms (1 lb/500 g)	1.5 L
1/4 tsp	hot pepper flakes	1 mL
	SAUCE	
1/3 cup	butter	75 mL
1/2 cup	all-purpose flour	125 mL
4 cups	milk	1 L
1 tsp	salt	5 mL
1/4 tsp	pepper	1 mL

● In large pot of boiling salted water, cook rigatoni for 8 to 10 minutes or until tender but firm. Drain and refresh under cold water. Drain well; set aside.

● MUSHROOM LAYER: In bowl, pour warm water over dried mushrooms; soak for 30 minutes. Drain, straining liquid through cheesecloth-lined sieve; set liquid aside. Rinse mushrooms and chop; set aside.

● In large skillet, melt butter over medium heat; cook onions for about 5 minutes or until softened. Add fresh mushrooms, chopped wild mushrooms and hot pepper flakes; cook for 2 minutes. Add reserved soaking liquid; cook, stirring often, for 20 minutes or until no liquid remains. Remove from heat; set aside.

● SAUCE: In large saucepan, melt butter over medium heat; whisk in flour and cook, without browning, for 3 minutes. Whisk in milk; bring to boil, stirring constantly. Add salt and pepper; reduce heat and simmer, stirring often, for 5 to 7 minutes or until thickened.

● Arrange half of the rigatoni in greased 13- x 9-inch (3 L) baking dish. Spread with half of the mushroom mixture, then half of the sauce; scatter half each of the Fontina, Gorgonzola and Parmesan over top. Repeat layers.

● Bake in 350°F (180°C) oven for 40 to 50 minutes or until golden and bubbling. Makes 6 to 8 servings.

Baked Chicken and Spinach Pasta ▼

2	pkg (each 10 oz/284 g) fresh spinach	2
3-1/2 cups	penne	875 mL
1/3 cup	freshly grated Parmesan cheese	75 mL

CHICKEN SAUCE

2 tbsp	butter	25 mL
1/2 cup	diced ham	125 mL
2	onions, chopped	2
2	cloves garlic, minced	2
1	carrot, diced	1
1	sweet red pepper, diced	1
1-1/4 lb	ground chicken	625 g
1	can (28 oz/796 mL) tomatoes, puréed	1
2 tbsp	tomato paste	25 mL
1 tbsp	dried basil	15 mL
1 tsp	salt	5 mL
1/4 tsp	pepper	1 mL

CHEESE SAUCE

3 tbsp	butter	45 mL
1/4 cup	all-purpose flour	50 mL
3 cups	milk	750 mL
1-1/2 cups	shredded mozzarella cheese	375 mL
3/4 tsp	salt	4 mL
1/4 tsp	each pepper and nutmeg	1 mL

● CHICKEN SAUCE: In Dutch oven, melt butter over medium-high heat; cook ham, onions, garlic, carrot and red pepper for 10 minutes or until vegetables are softened. Using slotted spoon, transfer to dish; set aside.

● In same pan, cook chicken over high heat, breaking up with spoon, for 5 minutes or until no longer pink. Return ham mixture to pan along with tomatoes, tomato paste, basil, salt and pepper; bring to boil. Reduce heat and simmer for 30 minutes or until thickened.

● Meanwhile, rinse spinach; shake off excess water. In stockpot, cover spinach and cook, with just the water clinging to leaves, over medium-high heat for about 5 minutes or just until wilted. Drain well and squeeze dry; chop coarsely and set aside.

● CHEESE SAUCE: In heavy saucepan, melt butter over medium heat. Stir in flour; cook, stirring, for 2 minutes, without browning. Whisk in milk and bring to boil; reduce heat to medium-low and simmer, stirring often, for 5 minutes or until thickened. Stir in mozzarella, salt, pepper and nutmeg.

● Meanwhile, in large pot of boiling salted water, cook penne for 8 to 10 minutes or until tender but firm. Drain and toss with chicken sauce; spoon into 13- x 9-inch (3 L) baking dish, smoothing top. Top with spinach, then cheese sauce; sprinkle with Parmesan. Bake in 375°F (190°C) oven for about 45 minutes or until golden and bubbling. Let stand for 15 minutes. Makes 12 servings.

T his up-to-date baked pasta is perfect for entertaining in the nineties — elegant yet effortless! Ground chicken in the sauce adds a taste surprise.

Asparagus Cannelloni ▶

Even in the spring, a baked pasta is welcome, especially when it highlights the season's most popular vegetable — tender asparagus.

22	precooked cannelloni tubes	22
1/4 cup	freshly grated Parmesan cheese	50 mL
	FILLING	
1-1/2 lb	asparagus	750 g
1/3 cup	creamy goat cheese (chèvre)	75 mL
1	egg	1
1-1/2 cups	ricotta cheese	375 mL
1/3 cup	shredded mozzarella cheese	75 mL
1/2 tsp	grated lemon rind	2 mL
4 tsp	lemon juice	20 mL
3	green onions, minced	3
3/4 tsp	salt	4 mL
Pinch	pepper	Pinch
	SAUCE	
1/4 cup	butter	50 mL
1/4 cup	all-purpose flour	50 mL
3 cups	hot milk	750 mL
1/4 cup	shredded mozzarella cheese	50 mL
1/2 tsp	nutmeg	2 mL
	Salt and pepper	

● FILLING: Break off tough stems from asparagus; reserve for another use. Peel stems; cut into 1-inch (2.5 cm) lengths. In saucepan of boiling salted water, cook asparagus for about 10 minutes or until tender; drain. Transfer to food processor or blender; purée.

● In large bowl, beat goat cheese until smooth; gradually beat in egg and ricotta. Stir in asparagus, mozzarella, lemon rind and juice, onions, salt and pepper until well blended. Spoon into piping bag fitted with large plain tip; pipe into cannelloni tubes. Arrange in single layer in greased 13- x 9-inch (3 L) baking dish.

● SAUCE: In saucepan, melt butter over low heat; stir in flour and cook, whisking constantly, for 1 minute. Remove from heat and whisk in milk. Bring to boil over medium-high heat, stirring constantly. Reduce heat and simmer for 2 minutes. Add mozzarella, nutmeg, and salt and pepper to taste, stirring until cheese has melted.

● Pour sauce over cannelloni. Sprinkle with Parmesan. *(Recipe can be prepared to this point, covered and refrigerated for up to 2 days.)* Bake in 350°F (180°C) oven for 30 to 40 minutes or until bubbling. If desired, broil for 2 to 3 minutes or until lightly browned. Makes 8 servings.

ASPARAGUS — A SURE SIGN OF SPRING!

Celebrate the arrival of spring with tender Canadian-grown asparagus.

● Select firm, straight, rich-green spears that are uniform in size and have closed tips. Stalks should be well rounded: ridges are a sign of age. The thicker the spear, the tastier and more tender it is.

● Refrigerate for up to 3 days by wrapping the base of the stalks in damp paper towels and placing them in a plastic bag. Or, stand them in 1 inch (2.5 cm) of water and cover with plastic bag.

● Brush gently under cold running water to remove sand. Hold spear with both hands and snap off end; the stalk will break at the point where the toughness stops.

● Cook asparagus by layering spears in wide saucepan of boiling salted water and cooking for 2 to 5 minutes or until tender-crisp. Or, cook in steamer basket over boiling water for the same time.

Macaroni and Cheese Oven Omelette

Thursday night and the crisper looks bare. Ditto the meat tray. Thank goodness for some pasta, eggs, cheese and a frozen vegetable in the freezer. Peas can replace the spinach, if desired; you'll need 1 cup (250 mL).

1 cup	macaroni	250 mL
1	pkg (10 oz/300 g) frozen spinach, thawed	1
1 tbsp	vegetable oil	15 mL
1	onion, chopped	1
3/4 tsp	salt	4 mL
1/2 tsp	pepper	2 mL
8	eggs, beaten	8
1-1/2 cups	shredded old Cheddar cheese	375 mL
1/4 cup	dry bread crumbs	50 mL
1/4 tsp	dried sage	1 mL

● In large pot of boiling salted water, cook macaroni for 8 to 10 minutes or until tender but firm; drain, reserving 1/2 cup (125 mL) cooking water.

● Meanwhile, in sieve, press out moisture from spinach; chop spinach and set aside. In 8-inch (20 cm) ovenproof skillet, heat oil over medium heat; cook onion, stirring, for 5 minutes or until softened. Remove from heat; stir in macaroni, spinach, salt and pepper.

● Combine eggs with 1 cup (250 mL) of the Cheddar and reserved cooking water; pour evenly over macaroni mixture. Sprinkle with remaining Cheddar, bread crumbs and sage.

● Bake in 350°F (180°C) oven for about 25 minutes or until puffed and knife inserted in center comes out clean. Makes 4 servings.

Cheese and Sausage Cannelloni

There are three things that have streamlined this robust pasta dish. First, fresh lasagna rectangles rolled around the filling replace fiddly-to-fill cannelloni tubes. The freshness of this pasta also eliminates the boiling step, and since the sausage and spaghetti sauce are already seasoned, fewer ingredients are needed to create a full-flavored dish.

2 tbsp	olive oil	25 mL
1	small onion, finely chopped	1
1	clove garlic, minced	1
1	each carrot and stalk celery, diced	1
3/4 tsp	dried basil	4 mL
1/4 tsp	salt	1 mL
Pinch	pepper	Pinch
1 lb	Italian sausage	500 g
1/3 cup	red wine	75 mL
2 tbsp	tomato paste	25 mL
3/4 cup	ricotta cheese	175 mL
1	egg	1
1	pkg (10 oz/300 g) frozen chopped spinach, thawed and squeezed dry	1
12	fresh lasagna rectangles (6- x 5-inches/15 x 12 cm)	12
1-1/2 cups	shredded mozzarella cheese	375 mL
4 cups	Fast and Easy Spaghetti Sauce (recipe, p. 70)	1 L
1/4 cup	freshly grated Parmesan cheese	50 mL

● In large skillet, heat oil over medium heat; cook onion, garlic, carrot and celery for about 5 minutes or until softened. Stir in basil, salt and pepper; cook, stirring, for 1 minute.

● Remove sausage from casings. Add to skillet; cook, breaking up into small pieces, for about 10 minutes or until no longer pink. Drain off fat. Stir in wine and tomato paste until combined. Remove from heat; let cool slightly. Stir in ricotta, egg and spinach.

● Arrange lasagna in single layer on work surface. Spoon 1/3 cup (75 mL) filling along one long edge of each rectangle. Sprinkle 1 cup (250 mL) of the mozzarella evenly over filling. Starting at long edge, roll up each into cylinder.

● Pour 1-1/2 cups (375 mL) of the spaghetti sauce into 13- x 9-inch (3 L) baking dish, spreading evenly. Nestle stuffed cylinders snugly on top. Pour remaining tomato sauce over top; sprinkle with Parmesan and remaining mozzarella.

● Cover loosely with foil; bake in 350°F (180°C) oven for 20 minutes; uncover and bake for 10 minutes longer or until golden and bubbling. Makes 6 servings.

Baked Vegetable Spaghetti

2 tbsp	olive oil	25 mL
2	large onions, chopped	2
3	cloves garlic, minced	3
4	zucchini, diced	4
1	each sweet green and yellow pepper, diced	1
1	eggplant, peeled and diced	1
2	cans (each 19 oz/540 mL) tomatoes	2
1	can (5-1/2 oz/156 mL) tomato paste	1
2 tsp	dried basil	10 mL
1 tsp	each dried oregano, granulated sugar and salt	5 mL
1/2 tsp	pepper	2 mL
1/4 tsp	dried thyme	1 mL
1 lb	spaghetti	500 g
1/4 cup	freshly grated Parmesan cheese	50 mL
	CHEESE SAUCE	
1/4 cup	butter	50 mL
1/4 cup	all-purpose flour	50 mL
2 cups	milk	500 mL
1 cup	shredded mozzarella cheese	250 mL
1/2 tsp	salt	2 mL
1/4 tsp	pepper	1 mL

● In Dutch oven, heat half of the oil over medium-high heat; cook onions, garlic, zucchini, sweet peppers and eggplant, stirring often, for 5 to 10 minutes or until starting to soften.

● Add tomatoes, tomato paste, basil, oregano, sugar, salt, pepper and thyme; bring to boil. Reduce heat and simmer for 25 to 30 minutes or until slightly thickened.

● CHEESE SAUCE: In saucepan, melt butter over medium heat; stir in flour and cook, whisking, for 2 minutes, without browning. Gradually whisk in milk and bring to boil; reduce heat to medium-low and cook, whisking, for about 10 minutes or until thickened. Stir in mozzarella, salt and pepper until melted.

● Meanwhile, in large pot of boiling salted water, cook spaghetti for 5 minutes or until almost tender but still firm. Drain and toss with remaining olive oil and vegetable mixture.

● Transfer spaghetti mixture to 13- x 9-inch (3 L) baking dish, spreading evenly. Spoon cheese sauce over top. Sprinkle with Parmesan. *(Spaghetti can be cooled, covered and refrigerated for up to 1 day or frozen for up to 2 weeks. Thaw in refrigerator for 48 hours. Add 10 minutes to baking time.)*

● Bake on baking sheet in 350°F (180°C) oven for about 1 hour or until golden and heated through. Makes 8 servings.

When serving a crowd, it's always a good idea to provide a vegetarian dish such as this three-layer casserole — spaghetti, summery ratatouille and mozzarella topping — for guests who don't eat meat.

FREEZING CASSEROLES

To freeze, let casserole cool thoroughly in refrigerator. Overwrap with plastic wrap and enclose in airtight plastic container or large freezer bag. To thaw, remove from container and place in refrigerator. Because casseroles are often dense, they take 1 to 2 days to thaw completely.

Pastitsio Pie ▶

Creamy custard-topped pastitsio is as soothing and satisfying as lasagna, with an added touch of the exotic — wisps of cinnamon in the beef sauce and nutmeg in the cheese custard.

1 tbsp	butter	15 mL
1	onion, chopped	1
3	cloves garlic, minced	3
1-1/2 lb	lean ground beef	750 g
1/2 tsp	each dried oregano, cinnamon and salt	2 mL
1/4 tsp	pepper	1 mL
1	can (14 oz/398 mL) stewed tomatoes	1
1	can (5-1/2 oz/156 mL) tomato paste	1
1 tbsp	red wine vinegar	15 mL
1/4 cup	chopped fresh parsley	50 mL
2 cups	macaroni	500 mL
2 tbsp	dry bread crumbs	25 mL
1 cup	freshly grated Parmesan cheese	250 mL
	SAUCE	
2 tbsp	butter	25 mL
2 tbsp	all-purpose flour	25 mL
1 cup	milk	250 mL
1 cup	cottage cheese	250 mL
1	egg	1
Pinch	each nutmeg, salt and pepper	Pinch

● In nonstick skillet, melt half of the butter over medium heat; cook onion and garlic, stirring, for 3 minutes. Stir in beef, oregano, cinnamon, salt and pepper; cook, stirring, for 7 to 10 minutes or until no longer pink. Drain off fat. Stir in tomatoes, tomato paste and vinegar; cook, stirring, for 3 minutes. Remove from heat; stir in parsley. Set aside.

● Meanwhile, in large pot of boiling salted water, cook macaroni for 8 to 10 minutes or until tender but firm. Drain and refresh under cold water; drain again and set aside.

● SAUCE: In saucepan, melt butter over medium heat; stir in flour and cook, whisking, for 2 minutes, without browning. Gradually whisk in milk and cook, whisking, for about 5 minutes or until thickened; remove from heat. Stir in cottage cheese, egg, nutmeg, salt and pepper.

● Grease 10-inch (25 cm) deep pie plate with remaining butter; sprinkle with bread crumbs. Spoon in half of the macaroni. Spread meat mixture evenly over top, pressing down lightly; sprinkle with one-third of the Parmesan.

● Spoon remaining macaroni over top; carefully pour sauce over macaroni. *(Pie can be covered and refrigerated for up to 1 day. Let stand at room temperature for 30 minutes; add 10 minutes to baking time.)*

● Sprinkle with remaining Parmesan. Bake on baking sheet in 350°F (180°C) oven for 50 to 60 minutes or until golden. Makes 6 servings.

Long Simmers

Time, and only time, can work its magic on flavors — mellowing here, concentrating there — to create sauces with exquisite depth and robust elegance.

Abruzzi-Style Spaghetti

Glen Antonacci, originator of this deliciously thick and smooth spaghetti sauce, uses tomato paste and juice instead of tomatoes — in the style of his home region of Abruzzi, Italy.

1-1/2 lb	pork spareribs	750 g
1 lb	Calabrian sausage with fennel seeds and paprika	500 g
3/4 cup	(approx) freshly grated Parmesan cheese	175 mL
1/2 cup	Italian-seasoned bread crumbs	125 mL
2 tbsp	dried basil	25 mL
4	cloves garlic, minced	4
1 tbsp	granulated sugar	15 mL
1/2 tsp	pepper	2 mL
1	can (48 oz/1.36 L) tomato juice	1
1	can (5-1/2 oz/156 mL) tomato paste	1
1-1/2 lb	spaghetti	750 g
	Chopped fresh parsley	

● Cut spareribs into 2- or 3-rib portions. Cut sausage into 3-inch (8 cm) lengths. Set aside.

● In large heavy saucepan or Dutch oven, combine cheese, bread crumbs, basil, garlic, sugar and pepper. Add tomato juice and paste, whisking to blend in paste.

● Add spareribs and sausage; bring to boil over medium heat. Reduce heat to very low and simmer, stirring occasionally, for about 2 hours or until thickened and meat is tender enough to fall off bones.

● Meanwhile, in large pot of boiling salted water, cook spaghetti for 8 to 10 minutes or until tender but firm; drain well.

● Remove sausage and spareribs; arrange around edge of warmed serving platter. Toss spaghetti with about 2 cups (500 mL) of the sauce; arrange in center of meat. Sprinkle with parsley and more cheese. Serve remaining sauce in pitcher alongside platter. Makes 6 to 8 servings.

TIP: Ingredients such as prosciutto (Italian ham) and pancetta (Italian bacon) are more widely available now that many Italian products have gone supermarket-mainstream. However, mild ham and lean bacon can replace them both, and any good fresh (not smoked or dried) Italian sausage can replace the Calabrian sausage.

STORING MEAT SAUCES

The first step to storing a meaty sauce is to chill it quickly. If there is a large quantity, transfer it to a large shallow airtight container and refrigerate it, uncovered, until completely cold. Cover and freeze, or use within a day or two or according to time recommended in recipe.

Tomato and Wild Mushroom Linguine

1	pkg (1/2 oz/15 g) dried wild mushrooms	1
1 tbsp	olive oil	15 mL
1	small onion, chopped	1
2	cloves garlic, minced	2
4	slices prosciutto, chopped	4
3 cups	sliced fresh mushrooms (12 oz/375 g)	750 mL
1	can (28 oz/796 mL) tomatoes, chopped	1
1 tsp	salt	5 mL
3/4 tsp	each pepper and dried thyme	4 mL
8 oz	linguine	250 g
	Freshly grated Parmesan cheese	

● Rinse dried mushrooms under cold water. Soak for 15 minutes in 1 cup (250 mL) boiling water. Strain through cheesecloth-lined sieve, reserving liquid. Rinse mushrooms and chop coarsely; set aside.

● In saucepan, heat oil over medium heat; cook onion, garlic and prosciutto, stirring, for 3 minutes or until onion is softened. Add fresh mushrooms and reserved soaking liquid; cook, stirring gently, for 10 to 15 minutes or until liquid is reduced to half.

● Stir in tomatoes, soaked mushrooms, salt, pepper and thyme; bring to boil. Reduce heat and simmer, stirring occasionally, for about 25 minutes or until thickened.

● Meanwhile, in large pot of boiling salted water, cook linguine for 8 to 10 minutes or until tender but firm; drain well. Toss with sauce; sprinkle with Parmesan to taste. Makes 2 servings.

A few dried porcini or morel mushrooms give a rich, woodsy taste to a pasta sauce. But if fresh mushrooms are all you have, by all means use fresh, adding another cup (250 mL) to the quantity in the recipe.

Spaghetti Bolognese

3 tbsp	vegetable oil	50 mL
1	onion, chopped	1
2	cloves garlic, minced	2
1	each carrot and stalk celery, finely diced	1
1 lb	ground beef	500 g
1 cup	white wine	250 mL
1/2 cup	milk	125 mL
1-1/4 tsp	salt	6 mL
3/4 tsp	pepper	4 mL
Pinch	nutmeg	Pinch
1	can (28 oz/796 mL) tomatoes, chopped	1
2 tbsp	tomato paste	25 mL
1	bay leaf	1
12 oz	spaghetti	375 g
	Freshly grated Parmesan cheese	
	Chopped fresh parsley	

● In large heavy saucepan, heat oil over medium-low heat; cook onion, garlic, carrot and celery, stirring, for about 5 minutes or until softened.

● Add beef; cook, stirring to break up, for about 10 minutes or just until no longer pink, being careful not to brown. Drain off fat.

● Pour in wine; increase heat to medium-high and cook, stirring occasionally, until wine has evaporated. Add milk, salt, pepper and nutmeg; cook, stirring, until milk has evaporated.

● Add tomatoes, tomato paste and bay leaf; bring to boil. Reduce heat to low and cook, stirring occasionally, for about 2 hours or until thickened. Discard bay leaf.

● Meanwhile, in large pot of boiling salted water, cook spaghetti for 8 to 10 minutes or until tender but firm; drain well.

● In warmed serving bowl, toss spaghetti with half of the sauce. Top with remaining sauce. Sprinkle with Parmesan and parsley to taste. Makes 4 servings.

This is ragu, the mother of all spaghetti sauces in Canada — and worth every minute it takes to simmer the beef with tomatoes, bay leaf and the surprise ingredient, milk. While unexpected here, milk is traditionally added in Italy because it keeps the meat deliciously tender through the long and slow simmering.

Italian Sausage and Tomato Fettuccine

The long simmer brings out the sweetness of the onion and carrot, tempering the acidity of the tomatoes. While the red wine is optional, it is recommended for the balance it brings to the sausage and vegetables.

3 tbsp	olive oil	50 mL
1	onion, chopped	1
2	cloves garlic, minced	2
1	each large carrot and stalk celery, finely diced	1
1 cup	sliced mushrooms (4 oz/125 g)	250 mL
1	sweet green pepper, chopped	1
2 tbsp	(approx) chopped fresh parsley	25 mL
2 tsp	dried basil	10 mL
1 tsp	salt	5 mL
3/4 tsp	pepper	4 mL
1 lb	Italian sausage with fennel seeds	500 g
1	can (28 oz/796 mL) tomatoes, chopped	1
1/2 cup	red wine (optional)	125 mL
1/4 cup	tomato paste	50 mL
12 oz	fettuccine or fusilli	375 g
	Freshly grated Parmesan cheese	

● In Dutch oven or large saucepan, heat oil over medium heat; cook onion, garlic, carrot, celery, mushrooms, green pepper, parsley, basil, salt and pepper for 3 to 5 minutes or until softened.

● Remove sausage from casings. Add to saucepan; cook, breaking up into small pieces, for 5 minutes or until no longer pink. Stir in tomatoes, wine (if using) and tomato paste; bring to boil. Reduce heat and simmer, stirring occasionally, for 1-1/2 hours or until thickened.

● Meanwhile, in large pot of boiling salted water, cook fettuccine for 8 to 10 minutes or until tender but firm; drain well.

● In warmed serving bowl, toss fettuccine with half of the sauce. Pour remaining sauce over top; sprinkle with Parmesan and more parsley to taste. Makes 4 servings.

TIP: If sausage with fennel seeds is unavailable in your area, use regular Italian sausage and add 1 tbsp (15 mL) crushed fennel seeds to the tomato sauce.

PAIRING PASTA WITH SAUCES

It's important to make a good match between pasta shapes and sauces. Where possible in our recipes, we have suggested several complementary pasta choices for a sauce. At the same time, we've left room for personal taste and preference, so do feel free to enjoy your favorite sauce with the pasta you like best!

● **Long, thin pastas** such as fettuccine and spaghetti work well with tomato, cream, and butter and cheese sauces; strong-flavored sauces with garlic or anchovies; and fish or seafood sauces.

● Team up **short, curled or twisted pasta** shapes such as fusilli, penne and conchiglie with meat or vegetable sauces because the pasta traps tasty morsels inside and you can pick up both the pasta and chunks of meat or vegetables at the same time.

● **Small pastas** such as macaroni are good in a minestrone or a soup with legumes.

● **Flat, short pastas** such as farfalle are best coated in a delicate cream, cheese or vegetable sauce.

Fusilli with Meatball Stew ▼

1	large onion, chopped	1
4	cloves garlic, minced	4
2-1/4 cups	halved mushrooms (8 oz/250 g)	550 mL
2 tsp	dried basil	10 mL
3/4 tsp	dried sage	4 mL
1/4 tsp	hot pepper flakes	1 mL
4 tsp	all-purpose flour	20 mL
1-1/2 cups	beef stock	375 mL
3 tbsp	tomato paste	50 mL
1 tbsp	red wine vinegar	15 mL
1	bay leaf	1
3	carrots, sliced	3
1/2 tsp	(approx) salt	2 mL
1	each sweet red and yellow pepper, chopped	1
1	zucchini, halved and sliced	1
1 cup	frozen peas	250 mL
	Pepper	
1 lb	fusilli lunghi	500 g

	MEATBALLS	
1-1/2 lb	lean ground beef	750 g
1	small onion, minced	1
1	egg	1
2 tbsp	freshly grated Parmesan cheese	25 mL
1 tsp	dried basil	5 mL
1/2 tsp	salt	2 mL
1/4 tsp	each dried sage and pepper	1 mL
4 tsp	vegetable oil	20 mL

● MEATBALLS: In bowl, combine beef, onion, egg, Parmesan, basil, salt, sage and pepper; shape into 18 meatballs. In Dutch oven, heat oil over medium-high heat; cook meatballs, turning often, for 8 to 12 minutes or until well browned. Drain on paper towel.

● Drain off all but 1 tbsp (15 mL) fat from pan; cook onion, garlic, mushrooms, basil, sage and hot pepper flakes, stirring, for about 3 minutes or until onion is softened.

● Sprinkle with flour; cook, stirring, for 1 minute. Gradually pour in stock, scraping up brown bits; bring to boil.

● Stir in tomato paste, vinegar, bay leaf, carrots and salt; add meatballs. Reduce heat to low and simmer, partially covered, for 20 to 30 minutes or until carrots are almost tender. Stir in red and yellow peppers; cook for 1 minute. *(Stew can be prepared to this point and refrigerated in airtight container for up to 1 day or frozen for up to 2 months; thaw and reheat over medium heat.)*

● Add zucchini and peas; simmer for 5 to 10 minutes or until tender. Discard bay leaf. Season with more salt and pepper to taste.

● Meanwhile, in large pot of boiling salted water, cook fusilli for 8 to 10 minutes or until tender but firm; drain well. Arrange on plates; top with stew. Makes 6 servings.

*W*arm up a cold evening with a simmered meatball-and-vegetable stew to serve over curly long fusilli. Pass freshly grated Parmesan to sprinkle on each serving.

Spaghetti with Meatballs

3/4 lb	ground beef	375 g
1	egg	1
1/4 cup	dry bread crumbs	50 mL
1/2 tsp	salt	2 mL
1/2 tsp	each dry mustard and basil	2 mL
1/4 tsp	pepper	1 mL
	Fast and Easy Spaghetti Sauce (recipe, this page)	
12 oz	spaghetti	375 g
1/4 cup	freshly grated Parmesan cheese	50 mL
2 tbsp	chopped fresh basil or parsley	25 mL

● In large bowl, mix together beef, egg, bread crumbs, salt, mustard, basil and pepper. Form into 1-inch (2.5 cm) meatballs; place on rimmed baking sheet.

● Bake in 400°F (200°C) oven for 15 to 20 minutes or until no longer pink inside. Drain off fat.

● In large saucepan, heat spaghetti sauce until simmering. Add meatballs and simmer for 10 minutes.

● Meanwhile, in large pot of boiling salted water, cook spaghetti for 8 to 10 minutes or until tender but firm; drain well and toss with Parmesan. Arrange on warmed serving platter; spoon sauce over top. Sprinkle with fresh basil. Makes 4 servings.

Fast and Easy Spaghetti Sauce

What to cook when the cupboard is almost bare? If there's some spaghetti and a big can of tomatoes, this to-the-rescue recipe offers a quick and delicious weeknight supper.

2 tbsp	olive oil	25 mL
1	onion, chopped	1
3	cloves garlic, minced	3
1	each carrot and stalk celery, diced	1
1-1/2 cups	sliced mushrooms (6 oz/175 g)	375 mL
1	sweet green pepper, chopped	1
1 tsp	dried basil	5 mL
3/4 tsp	salt	4 mL
Pinch	hot pepper flakes (optional)	Pinch
1	can (28 oz/796 mL) tomatoes, puréed	1
1/4 cup	tomato paste	50 mL

● In large saucepan, heat oil over medium-high heat; cook onion, garlic, carrot, celery, mushrooms and green pepper for 8 to 10 minutes or until softened.

● Stir in basil, salt, and hot pepper flakes (if using); cook, stirring, for 1 minute. Pour in tomatoes and tomato paste; bring to boil. Reduce heat and simmer for about 30 minutes or until thickened. Makes 4 cups (1 L).

THE BEST TOMATOES FOR SAUCE

When making a fresh tomato sauce, the best tomatoes to choose are plum tomatoes. These pear-shaped tomatoes are meatier and drier than round slicing tomatoes and make a thicker, tastier sauce in less time. Take a tip from Italian families who preserve tomatoes every summer — spread out garden-picked or store-bought plum tomatoes in a single layer to ripen fully to an intense red.

Winter's Big-Batch Tomato Sauce

2 tbsp	olive oil	25 mL
2 tbsp	chopped onions	25 mL
4	cloves garlic, minced	4
1 tsp	granulated sugar	5 mL
1 tsp	each dried basil, oregano and salt	5 mL
1/2 tsp	each dried thyme and pepper	2 mL
4	carrots, diced	4
2	stalks celery, chopped	2
1	sweet green pepper, chopped	1
3	cans (each 28 oz/796 mL) stewed tomatoes	3
1 cup	tomato paste	250 mL

● In large heavy saucepan, heat oil over medium heat; cook onions and garlic for 3 minutes or until softened.

● Stir in sugar, basil, oregano, salt, thyme and pepper. Add carrots, celery and green pepper; cook, stirring, for 3 minutes.

● Stir in tomatoes and tomato paste; bring to boil. Reduce heat and simmer, stirring occasionally, for 45 to 60 minutes or until thickened slightly. Makes 12 cups (3 L).

Even in winter, you can simmer a fine pasta sauce from scratch. This one makes enough to see you through three or four meals — a toss with pasta, a lasagna, a pizza or even a sauce for chicken or fish.

Summer's Fresh Herb Tomato Sauce

1/3 cup	olive oil	75 mL
3	stalks celery, chopped	3
2	large carrots, chopped	2
1	onion, chopped	1
1	large clove garlic, minced	1
9 lb	plum tomatoes (about 4 dozen)	4 kg
2 tsp	each chopped fresh basil and oregano	10 mL
1 tsp	granulated sugar	5 mL
1/2 tsp	salt	2 mL
1/4 tsp	pepper	1 mL
1/4 tsp	fennel seeds	1 mL
1	bay leaf	1

● In large heavy saucepan or Dutch oven, heat oil over medium heat; cook celery, carrots, onion and garlic, stirring often, for 15 minutes or until tender but not browned.

● Trim, core and coarsely chop tomatoes; add to pan and bring to simmer. Cook, mashing occasionally, for 45 to 60 minutes or until vegetables are tender. Pass through medium disk of food mill or through conical ricer; pour into large clean saucepan.

● Add basil, oregano, sugar, salt, pepper, fennel seeds and bay leaf; bring to simmer. Cook, stirring frequently, for 1-1/2 to 2 hours or until thickened. Discard bay leaf.

● Pour sauce into airtight containers, leaving 1/2-inch (1 cm) headspace; freeze. Makes about 12 cups (3 L).

Summertime — and the garden is overflowing. Why not freeze a taste of the harvest to enjoy all winter long? For convenience, freeze this summer-fresh sauce in quantities that suit your household's favorite recipes.

Putting up Tomatoes ▶

Nothing can beat the convenience and taste of home-canned tomatoes — ready to simmer into a sauce, or toss into a soup or stew. Here's how to capture the summer harvest in a cannerful of tomatoes that will last all winter long.

18 lb	firm ripe tomatoes (about 8 dozen plum or 4 dozen round)	8 kg
	Citric acid or reconstituted lemon juice	

● Wash and rinse canning jars and bands. About 45 minutes before filling jars, fill boiling water bath canner two-thirds full of water; heat to just below boil and keep hot.

● Place jars in rack set on edge of canner or in 225°F (110°C) oven to heat. A few minutes before filling jars, bring pot of water to boil; boil lids for 5 minutes. Remove from heat; leave in water until ready to use.

● In large pot of boiling water, blanch tomatoes, in batches, for 30 to 60 seconds or until skins loosen. Remove and chill in cold water; drain immediately and peel. Core and trim away any green, bruised or decayed spots; cut into quarters.

● In two large pots or in batches, over high heat, heat tomatoes until heated through and juices boil, about 10 minutes.

● Filling one jar at a time, pack tomatoes and juice into jar, leaving 1/2-inch (or 2 cm) headspace. For each 4-cup (1 L) jar, add 1/2 tsp (2 mL) citric acid or 2 tbsp (25 mL) reconstituted lemon juice. (For each 2 cup/500 mL jar, add 1/4 tsp/1 mL citric acid or 1 tbsp/15 mL reconstituted lemon juice.)

● Run spatula around inside of jar, pressing tomatoes to release any air bubbles. Add more tomatoes or juice if needed to maintain 1/2-inch (or 2 cm) headspace.

● With clean damp cloth, wipe rim. Cover with lid; screw on band firmly without forcing (fingertip tight). Place on rack set on edge of canner. Lower filled rack into water.

● Pour in enough simmering water, avoiding tops of jars, to cover jars by 1 to 2 inches (2.5 to 5 cm). Cover canner and bring to full rolling boil. Boil 4-cup (1 L) jars for 45 minutes, 2-cup (500 mL) jars for 35 minutes. Turn off heat.

● Lift rack to sit on edge of canner. Using jar lifter, transfer jars to towel-lined surface. Let cool completely (some separation of juice in jars is natural). Do not retighten screw bands.

● Check for seal to ensure lids curve inward and don't move when pressed with finger. Refrigerate any improperly sealed jars; use within 3 days. Store in cool, dark, dry place. Store in refrigerator after opening. Makes about 28 cups (7 L).

FOR BEST RESULTS

● Letting tomatoes ripen fully before canning (see sidebar, p. 70) makes for a richer-colored and tastier home-canned product. Plum tomatoes are best since they are less watery than the beefsteak variety and cook up into a thicker, more flavorful sauce. Be sure to can only firm ripe tomatoes, not overripe, soft ones.

● It is safe to can tomatoes in a boiling water canner; other vegetables require pressure canning. Don't add vegetables when canning tomatoes; add them when preparing a dish.

● Always use new lids. Reuse bands if not bent or rusty. Use canning jars that are free of nicks and cracks.

Magnifico Salads

Main dish, side dish, make-ahead or last-minute toss — pasta salads are sensational any way you serve them. Here's our pick of the classics plus the hottest new tastes.

Antipasto Fusilli Salad

This simple salad has lots of old-fashioned Italian flavor. It also travels well, making it ideal for picnics or for the cottage. Tricolor pasta adds color.

3 cups	fusilli	750 mL
1/2 cup	extra virgin olive oil	125 mL
1/4 cup	white wine vinegar	50 mL
2 tbsp	water	25 mL
1/2 tsp	each dried oregano, basil and dry mustard	2 mL
1/4 tsp	each dried rosemary and black pepper	1 mL
1	clove garlic, minced	1
1	can (19 oz/540 mL) chick-peas or kidney beans, drained and rinsed	1
1	each carrot and zucchini, finely diced	1
1/2 cup	freshly grated Parmesan cheese	125 mL
	Salt	
	Lettuce leaves	
1 cup	cherry tomatoes	250 mL

● In large pot of boiling salted water, cook fusilli for 8 to 10 minutes or until tender but firm; drain well.

● Meanwhile, in large bowl, whisk together oil, vinegar, water, oregano, basil, mustard, rosemary, pepper and garlic. Stir in warm pasta to coat thoroughly.

● Add chick-peas, carrot, zucchini, Parmesan, and salt to taste. *(Salad can be refrigerated for up to 1 day.)* Spoon onto lettuce-lined plates; top with tomatoes. Makes 6 servings.

Greek Pasta Salad

Bow-tie pasta (farfalle) is an excellent choice for salads — it's firm enough to withstand cooking, tossing and a day in the refrigerator without getting mushy.

8 cups	farfalle	2 L
1/2 cup	extra virgin olive oil	125 mL
1/3 cup	lemon juice	75 mL
1 tbsp	anchovy paste	15 mL
2	cloves garlic, minced	2
1 tsp	dried oregano	5 mL
Pinch	each salt and pepper	Pinch
1	small cucumber	1
2 cups	small cherry tomatoes	500 mL
1 cup	small black olives	250 mL
1 cup	chopped red onion	250 mL
1/2 cup	chopped fresh parsley	125 mL
1 cup	finely diced feta cheese (about 4 oz/125 g)	250 mL

● In large pot of boiling salted water, cook farfalle for 8 to 10 minutes or until tender but firm; drain well.

● Meanwhile, whisk together oil, lemon juice, anchovy paste, garlic, oregano, salt and pepper; toss half with pasta. Let cool to room temperature, stirring occasionally.

● Cut cucumber in half lengthwise. Scoop out seeds and thinly slice crosswise. Add to pasta along with tomatoes, olives, onion, parsley and remaining dressing; toss to coat well. Gently stir in feta cheese. *(Salad can be covered and refrigerated for up to 1 day.)* Makes about 10 servings.

Choose-Your-Fish Pasta Salad ▲

3 cups	rotini	750 mL
1	can (19 oz/540 mL) red kidney beans, drained and rinsed	1
4	green onions, chopped	4
2	sweet green peppers, chopped	2
1/2 cup	sliced black olives	125 mL
2	cans (each 7-1/2 oz/213 g) salmon or tuna (or 2 cups/500 mL flaked grilled or cooked fish)	2
2	tomatoes, chopped	2
1	head leaf lettuce or 2 bunches watercress	1
	DRESSING	
1/3 cup	red wine vinegar	75 mL
1/4 cup	lemon juice	50 mL
3	large cloves garlic, minced	3
1 tbsp	dried oregano	15 mL
1 tsp	salt	5 mL
1/2 tsp	pepper	2 mL
1/2 cup	extra virgin olive oil	125 mL

● In large pot of boiling salted water, cook rotini for 8 to 10 minutes or until tender but firm. Drain and refresh under cold water; drain well.

● DRESSING: Meanwhile, in small bowl, combine vinegar, lemon juice, garlic, oregano, salt and pepper; gradually whisk in oil.

● In large bowl, combine pasta, beans, green onions, green peppers and olives; toss lightly with half of the dressing. *(Salad can be prepared to this point, covered and refrigerated for up to 1 day.)*

● Drain salmon and break up into chunks; add to bowl along with tomatoes and remaining dressing. Toss lightly. Line plates with lettuce; top with salad. Makes 6 servings.

It's your pick — tuna, salmon or leftover cooked fish — in this colorful red bean and rotini salad.

Ham and Artichoke Heart Salad

Summer — and with a big bowl of pasta salad, meal-making certainly is easy. If you want to pack this salad for a picnic, don't chop and mix in the tomato until you're ready to eat.

2-1/2 cups	penne	625 mL
2 cups	chopped green beans	500 mL
1	large tomato	1
1	sweet red pepper	1
6	green onions	6
1	jar (6 oz/170 mL) marinated artichoke hearts	1
8 oz	cooked ham, cut into strips	250 g
	Pepper	
2 tbsp	chopped fresh parsley	25 mL
	DRESSING	
1/4 cup	cider vinegar	50 mL
1 tbsp	grainy mustard	15 mL
2 tsp	Dijon mustard	10 mL
1	clove garlic, minced	1
1/2 tsp	salt	2 mL
1/2 cup	extra virgin olive oil	125 mL

● In large pot of boiling salted water, cook penne for 7 minutes. Add green beans; cook for 3 minutes or until tender-crisp and pasta is tender but firm. Drain and refresh under cold water; drain well and place in large bowl.

● Meanwhile, coarsely chop tomato. Seed and cut red pepper in half crosswise; cut into thin strips. Slice green onions. Drain artichoke hearts, reserving 1 tbsp (15 mL) marinade; cut hearts in half.

● Add tomato, red pepper, green onions, artichoke hearts and ham to pasta mixture.

● DRESSING: In small bowl, whisk together vinegar, grainy and Dijon mustards, garlic and salt; gradually whisk in oil. Whisk in reserved artichoke marinade. Pour over salad; toss gently to combine. Season with pepper to taste. Garnish with parsley. Makes 4 to 6 servings.

Garden Pasta Salad

Dressings for pasta salads need lots of flavor, and two kinds of mustard (grainy and Dijon) provide it here. Sturdy short pasta such as rotelle (cartwheel shapes) is the best choice for salads.

2	carrots, sliced	2
1	sweet red pepper, thinly sliced	1
Half	red onion, coarsely chopped	Half
1	head broccoli	1
1	zucchini	1
2-1/2 cups	rotelle	625 mL
	DRESSING	
1 cup	plain yogurt	250 mL
2 tbsp	Dijon mustard	25 mL
1 tbsp	grainy mustard	15 mL
1	clove garlic, minced	1
1/4 tsp	each salt and pepper	1 mL
Pinch	granulated sugar	Pinch
2 tbsp	chopped fresh basil or parsley	25 mL

● Place carrots, red pepper and onion in large salad bowl.

● Cut broccoli into bite-size florets; reserve stalks for another use. Cut zucchini in half lengthwise; slice crosswise.

● In large pot of boiling salted water, cook rotelle for 7 minutes. Add broccoli; cook for 2 minutes. Add zucchini; cook for 1 minute. Drain and refresh under cold water; drain well and add to vegetables in bowl.

● DRESSING: Stir together yogurt, Dijon and grainy mustards, garlic, salt, pepper and sugar; pour over vegetables and toss gently. Sprinkle with basil. Makes 4 to 6 servings.

TIP: This refreshing salad is also wonderful with a variety of add-ins — 1 can of drained tuna, 2 cups (500 mL) leftover cooked flaked salmon, 2 cups (500 mL) julienned ham or 1-1/2 cups (375 mL) cubed cheese.

Grilled Vegetable and Fusilli Salad

1	each sweet red, green and yellow pepper	1
2	zucchini	2
12 oz	mushrooms	375 g
1	red onion	1
1/4 cup	vegetable oil	50 mL
2-1/3 cups	fusilli	575 mL
	DRESSING	
1/3 cup	chopped fresh basil	75 mL
1/4 cup	red wine vinegar	50 mL
1 tbsp	Dijon mustard	15 mL
2	cloves garlic, minced	2
3/4 tsp	each salt and pepper	4 mL
1/2 cup	extra virgin olive oil	125 mL

● Place red, green and yellow peppers on greased grill over medium-high heat; cook, turning often, for 20 to 25 minutes or until charred. Let cool slightly; peel, seed and cut into thick strips. Place in large bowl.

● Meanwhile, cut zucchini diagonally into 1/2-inch (1 cm) thick slices. Trim stems from mushrooms. Cut onion into 8 wedges. Lightly brush vegetables with oil.

● Place mushrooms and onion on grill; cook, turning occasionally, for 8 to 10 minutes or until tender. Remove and set aside. Place zucchini on grill; cook for 10 to 15 minutes or until tender. Cut mushrooms, onions and zucchini into quarters. Add to sweet peppers in bowl.

● DRESSING: In small bowl, whisk together basil, vinegar, mustard, garlic, salt and pepper; gradually whisk in oil. Pour over vegetables; marinate for at least 8 hours or up to 24 hours.

● In large pot of boiling salted water, cook fusilli for 8 to 10 minutes or until tender but firm. Drain and refresh under cold water; drain well and toss with vegetable mixture. Makes 4 servings.

Grilled peppers, zucchini and mushrooms add a new twist to pasta salad. Garnish with fresh basil leaves and cherry tomatoes.

Pasta Salad Niçoise

3 cups	penne or fusilli	750 mL
2	tomatoes, coarsely chopped	2
1	sweet green or yellow pepper, cut into strips	1
Half	red onion, sliced	Half
1	can (7 oz/198 g) tuna, drained and broken into chunks	1
1/2 cup	sliced black olives	125 mL
2 tbsp	chopped fresh basil	25 mL
	Pepper	
2	hard-cooked eggs	2
	DRESSING	
3 tbsp	red wine vinegar	50 mL
1 tbsp	lemon juice	15 mL
1 tsp	Dijon mustard	5 mL
1/2 tsp	salt	2 mL
1	clove garlic, minced	1
1/3 cup	extra virgin olive oil	75 mL

● In large pot of boiling salted water, cook penne for 8 to 10 minutes or until tender but firm. Drain and refresh under cold water; drain well and place in salad bowl. Add tomatoes, green pepper, onion, tuna and olives.

● DRESSING: In small bowl, whisk together vinegar, lemon juice, mustard, salt and garlic; gradually whisk in oil. Pour over pasta mixture; add basil and toss gently to combine. Season with pepper to taste. Quarter eggs; arrange over salad. Makes 4 servings.

A Niçoise salad usually includes potatoes, but this pasta variation is a delicious change. (See photo on back cover, top right.)

Curried Chicken Pasta Salad

Chicken salad is like a story that gets told over and over again because everyone likes it — and each time, it's a little different. Here, it's exotic with a curry-yogurt dressing and radiatore (radiator-shaped) pasta.

1 tbsp	vegetable oil	15 mL
1 tsp	curry powder	5 mL
1 tsp	liquid honey	5 mL
4	boneless skinless chicken breasts	4
2-1/2 cups	radiatore	625 mL
1	large sweet green pepper, chopped	1
3	carrots, sliced	3
4	green onions, sliced	4
1/3 cup	currants	75 mL
1/2 cup	chopped toasted almonds (see p. 25)	125 mL
	DRESSING	
3/4 cup	plain yogurt	175 mL
3/4 cup	buttermilk	175 mL
1 tsp	curry powder	5 mL
1 tsp	liquid honey	5 mL
1/4 tsp	each dry mustard and ground coriander	1 mL
1/4 tsp	each salt and pepper	1 mL
Pinch	cinnamon	Pinch
3 tbsp	chopped fresh coriander	50 mL

● In small bowl, stir together oil, curry powder and honey; brush over one side of chicken breasts. Place on greased grill over medium-high heat; cook, turning once and brushing other side with remaining honey mixture, for 12 to 14 minutes or until no longer pink inside. Let cool slightly; cut into bite-size strips.

● Meanwhile, in large pot of boiling salted water, cook radiatore for 8 to 10 minutes or until tender but firm. Drain and refresh under cold water; drain well.

● In large salad bowl, combine radiatore, green pepper, carrots, green onions, currants and chicken.

● DRESSING: In separate bowl, stir together yogurt, buttermilk, curry powder, honey, mustard, ground coriander, salt, pepper and cinnamon. Stir in 2 tbsp (25 mL) of the chopped coriander. Pour over salad; toss gently to combine. Garnish with remaining coriander and almonds. Makes 4 to 6 servings.

Chicken and Tomato Pasta Salad

Leftover grilled chicken is sensational in a pasta salad, especially with summer-fresh basil and tomatoes.

4 cups	penne	1 L
2 cups	trimmed snow peas	500 mL
2	large tomatoes	2
1/3 cup	light mayonnaise	75 mL
1/4 cup	buttermilk	50 mL
1	clove garlic, minced	1
1/4 tsp	each salt and pepper	1 mL
2	cooked chicken breasts, cut into chunks	2
1/3 cup	chopped fresh basil	75 mL
	Fresh basil leaves	

● In large pot of boiling salted water, cook penne for 8 to 10 minutes or until tender but firm. Add snow peas; cook for 1 minute. Drain and refresh under cold water; drain well.

● Meanwhile, core tomatoes. Chop one tomato coarsely and set aside. Quarter remaining tomato; purée in food processor or blender. Add mayonnaise, buttermilk, garlic, salt and pepper; purée until smooth.

● In large bowl, toss together dressing, pasta mixture, reserved tomato, chicken and chopped basil. Garnish with basil leaves. Makes 4 servings.

Grilled Chicken and Noodle Salad ▼

2 cups	trimmed snow peas	500 mL
4	boneless skinless chicken breasts	4
1 tbsp	vegetable oil	15 mL
8 oz	buckwheat noodles*	250 g
2 cups	bean sprouts	500 mL
1/2 cup	unsalted roasted peanuts, chopped	125 mL
1/2 cup	slivered Spanish onion	125 mL
1/4 cup	snipped chives or green onions (green part only)	50 mL
	Tamari*	
	DRESSING	
2/3 cup	light mayonnaise	150 mL
1/4 cup	water	50 mL
3 tbsp	tahini*	45 mL
3 tbsp	tamari	45 mL
4 tsp	sesame oil	20 mL
Dash	hot pepper sauce	Dash

● DRESSING: Whisk together mayonnaise, water, tahini, tamari, sesame oil and hot pepper sauce. *(Dressing can be covered and refrigerated for up to 1 day.)*

● In pot of boiling water, cook snow peas for 1 minute or until tender-crisp. Drain and refresh under cold water; pat dry. *(Snow peas can be wrapped in tea towel and refrigerated for up to 8 hours.)*

● Brush chicken with oil; cook on greased grill over medium-high heat, turning once, for 12 to 15 minutes or until no longer pink inside. Let cool slightly; slice thinly on diagonal.

● Meanwhile, in large pot of boiling salted water, cook noodles for 5 minutes or until tender but firm. Drain and refresh under cold water; drain again. *(Noodles can be set aside in bowl of cold water in refrigerator for up to 2 hours; drain.)*

● In bowl, toss together dressing, noodles, bean sprouts, peanuts, onion, chives and snow peas. In middle of each salad plate, drizzle about 1 tsp (5 mL) tamari; mound noodle mixture on top. Fan chicken around noodle mixture. Makes 4 servings.

* Buckwheat noodles (soba), tahini (sesame paste) and tamari (soy sauce) are available at some specialty and health food stores.

W*oolfy's restaurant in Stratford, Ontario, is the source of this satisfying make-ahead salad. If you can't find buckwheat noodles (soba), you can use whole wheat spaghetti with delicious results.*

Old-Fashioned Macaroni Salad

Here's old-fashioned flavor with some new-fashioned, lower-fat ingredients such as light mayonnaise and low-fat yogurt or sour cream.

2-1/2 cups	macaroni	625 mL
2	each carrots and stalks celery, finely diced	2
1	sweet red pepper, finely diced	1
4	green onions, finely chopped	4
1 cup	shredded mozzarella cheese	250 mL
1/2 cup	finely chopped dill pickles	125 mL
1/4 cup	chopped fresh parsley	50 mL
	DRESSING	
1 cup	light mayonnaise	250 mL
3/4 cup	plain yogurt or low-fat sour cream	175 mL
2 tbsp	Dijon mustard	25 mL
1 tbsp	lemon juice	15 mL
1/4 tsp	each salt and pepper	1 mL

● In large pot of boiling salted water, cook macaroni for 8 to 10 minutes or until tender but firm. Drain and refresh under cold water until thoroughly chilled; drain well.

● In large bowl, combine macaroni, carrots, celery, red pepper, green onions, mozzarella and pickles.

● DRESSING: Stir together mayonnaise, yogurt, mustard, lemon juice, salt and pepper. Pour over macaroni mixture; toss gently until thoroughly combined. Garnish with parsley. Makes 4 servings.

Winter Vegetable Pasta Toss

Preparation of the pasta and winter vegetables for this hearty warm salad is simplified by cooking them together in one pot.

8 oz	butternut squash	375 g
1-1/2 cups	julienned peeled rutabaga or carrots	375 mL
2-3/4 cups	farfalle	675 mL
5	green onions, chopped	5
1/4 cup	chopped fresh parsley	50 mL
	Salt and pepper	
	VINAIGRETTE	
1/4 cup	apple juice	50 mL
3 tbsp	canola oil	45 mL
2 tbsp	cider vinegar	25 mL
1 tbsp	Dijon mustard	15 mL
Pinch	each salt and pepper	Pinch

● VINAIGRETTE: In small bowl, whisk together apple juice, oil, vinegar, mustard, salt and pepper; set aside.

● Peel and cut squash into 1- x 1/2-inch (2.5 x 1 cm) pieces; set aside.

● In large pot of boiling salted water, cook rutabaga and farfalle for 5 minutes. Add squash; cook for 6 to 7 minutes or just until vegetables are tender and pasta is tender but firm. Drain well.

● Toss pasta mixture with vinaigrette, green onions and parsley. Season with salt and pepper to taste. Makes 4 servings.

TIP: To julienne rutabaga or carrots, cut into sticks about 2 inches (5 cm) long and the thickness of a pencil.

Pack-and-Go Rotini Salad ▲

1/2 cup	extra virgin olive oil	125 mL
4	cloves garlic, minced	4
8 cups	rotini	2 L
1/2 cup	finely chopped fresh basil	125 mL
1	sweet yellow pepper, diced	1
1 cup	mild or medium salsa	250 mL
1 tbsp	red wine vinegar	15 mL
	Salt and pepper	
4	firm ripe tomatoes	4

● In small saucepan, combine 1/4 cup (50 mL) of the oil with garlic; heat over low heat for 5 minutes or until fragrant.

● Meanwhile, in large pot of boiling salted water, cook rotini for 8 to 10 minutes or until tender but firm; drain well.

● In large bowl, toss pasta with garlic mixture and remaining oil. Add basil, yellow pepper, salsa and vinegar; toss well. Season with salt and pepper to taste. Let cool completely. (*Salad can be prepared to this point, covered and refrigerated for up to 1 day.*)

● Halve and seed tomatoes; cut into large cubes. Toss with salad just before serving. Makes 12 servings.

This is a great salad to make for a reunion picnic or big barbecue buffet. Just add the tomatoes at serving time.

Broccoli and Rotini Salad ▲

This main-course salad is equally good warm or at room temperature.

2	bunches broccoli (2 lb/1 kg)	2
6 cups	rotini or penne	1.5 L
1/4 cup	raisins	50 mL
1/2 cup	extra virgin olive oil	125 mL
4	cloves garlic, minced	4
1/4 tsp	hot pepper flakes	1 mL
3	anchovy fillets, minced	3
1/3 cup	toasted pine nuts	75 mL
2 tbsp	chopped fresh basil	25 mL
1 tbsp	lemon juice	15 mL
	Salt and pepper	

● Cut broccoli into 2-inch (5 cm) pieces. In large pot of boiling salted water, cook broccoli for 5 to 8 minutes or until tender.

Remove with slotted spoon and refresh under cold water; drain, pat dry and transfer to large serving bowl.

● Add rotini to water in pot; cook for 8 to 10 minutes or until tender but firm. Drain and refresh under cold water; drain well. Add to broccoli.

● Meanwhile, in small bowl, cover raisins with boiling water. Let stand for 20 minutes; drain.

● In skillet, heat oil over low heat; cook garlic, hot pepper flakes and anchovies, stirring, for 3 to 4 minutes or until garlic is tender. Let cool slightly; add to pasta mixture. Add raisins, pine nuts, basil, lemon juice, and salt and pepper to taste; toss to combine. Makes 6 servings.

Buckwheat Noodle Salad

6	dried shiitake mushrooms	6
1 tbsp	tamari (see p.79) or soy sauce	15 mL
8 oz	buckwheat noodles or whole wheat spaghetti	250 g
1 tbsp	sesame oil	15 mL
1	English cucumber, diced	1
1/2 cup	chopped walnuts	125 mL
3 tbsp	chopped fresh coriander or parsley	50 mL
1	head leaf lettuce, separated	1
1/2 cup	sliced radishes	125 mL
	DRESSING	
2 tbsp	tahini (see p. 79) or crunchy peanut butter	25 mL
2 tbsp	tamari or soy sauce	25 mL
1/4 cup	cider vinegar	50 mL
2 tbsp	sesame oil	25 mL
1 tbsp	minced gingerroot	15 mL
1/2 tsp	hot pepper flakes	2 mL
1/4 tsp	pepper	1 mL
1	clove garlic, minced	1

● DRESSING: In small bowl, whisk together tahini and tamari until smooth. Whisk in vinegar, oil, ginger, hot pepper flakes, pepper and garlic; set aside.

● In separate small bowl, cover mushrooms with boiling water; stir in tamari. Let stand for 15 minutes. Drain and rinse well; discard stems. Slice caps into slivers.

● Meanwhile, in large pot of boiling salted water, cook noodles for 5 minutes or until tender but firm. Drain and refresh under cold water; drain well.

● In bowl, toss noodles with oil. Add mushrooms, cucumber, walnuts, coriander and dressing; toss well.

● Line salad bowl or platter with lettuce; top with noodle mixture. Garnish with radishes. Makes 6 servings.

East meets West in an appetizing blend of exotic and fresh flavors. This vegetarian main-course salad is a fine buffet dish.

Pesto Spaghetti Salad

1 lb	spaghetti or fusilli lunghi	500 g
5	carrots, sliced	5
2 cups	cauliflower florets	500 mL
2	sweet red, yellow or green peppers, cut into chunks	2
1 cup	Presto Pesto (recipe, p. 19)	250 mL

● In large pot of boiling salted water, cook spaghetti for 5 minutes. Add carrots, cauliflower and red pepper; cook for 5 minutes or until tender-crisp and spaghetti is tender but firm. Drain and refresh under cold water; drain well and place in bowl.

● Add Presto Pesto and toss to combine. *(Salad can be refrigerated for up to 8 hours.)* Makes 4 servings.

Green and cool for a summer supper, this salad can be made with whatever summer vegetables you fancy. Serve sliced cold meat or devilled eggs alongside.

Thai Vegetable Noodles

10	snow peas	10
12 oz	spaghetti	375 g
1	sweet red pepper, diced	1
1/2 cup	sliced water chestnuts, julienned	125 mL
1/3 cup	shredded fresh basil	75 mL
1/4 cup	chopped green onion	50 mL
Half	can (14 oz/398 mL) baby corn cobs, drained	Half
2 tbsp	toasted sesame seeds (see TIP, this page)	25 mL
	DRESSING	
1/3 cup	rice vinegar or white wine vinegar	75 mL
1/3 cup	hoisin sauce	75 mL
3 tbsp	each vegetable and sesame oil	45 mL
3 tbsp	soy sauce	45 mL
1 tbsp	minced gingerroot	15 mL
1-1/2 tsp	dry mustard	7 mL
1-1/2 tsp	granulated sugar	7 mL
2	cloves garlic, minced	2

● DRESSING: In bowl, whisk together vinegar, hoisin sauce, vegetable and sesame oils, soy sauce, ginger, mustard, sugar and garlic; set aside.

● In large pot of boiling water, blanch snow peas for 1 minute. Remove with slotted spoon and refresh under cold water; pat dry. Set aside.

● Add spaghetti to boiling water; cook for 8 to 10 minutes or until tender but firm. Drain well.

● In large bowl, toss together warm spaghetti, red pepper, water chestnuts, basil, onion, snow peas and two-thirds of the dressing; let cool slightly, about 5 minutes.

● Add remaining dressing; toss to mix. Garnish with baby corn cobs and sesame seeds. Makes 6 servings.

Spaghetti goes Oriental with water chestnuts and a zesty rice vinegar dressing. This moist salad is best served warm.

Spicy Sesame Noodles ◀

1-1/4 lb	fresh Chinese wheat noodles	625 g
1/4 cup	toasted sesame seeds (see TIP, this page)	50 mL
1/3 cup	chicken stock	75 mL
1/4 cup	soy sauce	50 mL
3 tbsp	rice vinegar	45 mL
4 tsp	hoisin sauce	20 mL
1 tbsp	chili oil (or 1/2 tsp/2 mL hot pepper sauce)	15 mL
2 tsp	sesame oil	10 mL
1/2 tsp	granulated sugar	2 mL
1/4 tsp	pepper	1 mL
Half	each cucumber and cantaloupe	Half
6	green onions, chopped	6
1/2 cup	chopped fresh coriander	125 mL
1/3 cup	chopped toasted walnuts	75 mL

● In large pot of boiling salted water, cook noodles for 5 to 7 minutes or until tender but firm. Drain and refresh under cold water; drain well and set aside.

● In bowl, combine sesame seeds, stock, soy sauce, rice vinegar, hoisin sauce, chili oil, sesame oil, sugar and pepper; add noodles and toss. Arrange on platter.

● Peel, seed and julienne cucumber and cantaloupe. Sprinkle over noodle mixture along with onions, coriander and walnuts. Makes 8 servings.

TIP: To toast sesame seeds, cook in small skillet over medium heat, stirring, for 3 to 6 minutes or until golden.

Melon and cucumber add freshness to a tangy, chili-spiked tangle of noodles. Toast walnuts in a skillet after the sesame seeds.

Making Fresh Pasta

Making your own pasta takes a little time, but you'll find the delicious fresh taste is worth every crank of the pasta machine. If you don't have a pasta machine, get out your rolling pin and follow our hand-rolled method. All of these pastas are scrumptious tossed with grated cheese, fresh herbs and butter — or see PRESTO PASTAS *for tasty inspirations.*

HAND-ROLLED FRESH PASTA

You can make your own fresh pasta even if you don't have a pasta machine.

● Prepare dough as outlined in steps 1 and 2 below.

● Follow step 3 and let dough rest for 1 hour before rolling out each piece with rolling pin to 1/16-inch (1.5 mm) thickness, rotating dough often and lightly dusting with flour to prevent sticking.

● Follow step 6.

● Roll up dough jelly roll-style into flat roll about 4 inches (10 cm) wide. Using sharp knife, cut roll crosswise into 1/4-inch (5 mm) wide strips. Unroll strips.

2 cups	all-purpose flour	500 mL
3	eggs	3
1/4 tsp	salt	1 mL

VARIATIONS

SPINACH PASTA: Cook 4 cups (1 L) trimmed fresh spinach until wilted. Drain, let cool and squeeze dry; chop finely to make about 1/3 cup (75 mL). Reduce eggs to 2. Add spinach to eggs and salt; mix well before incorporating flour.

SAFFRON PASTA: Add 1/8 tsp (0.5 mL) ground saffron to eggs and salt; mix well before incorporating flour.

ROASTED RED PEPPER PASTA: Broil 1 sweet red pepper, turning several times, for about 20 minutes or until blistered and charred. Let cool; peel, seed and chop finely. In food processor or blender, purée to make about 1/3 cup (75 mL). Reduce eggs to 2. Add purée to eggs and salt; mix well before incorporating flour.

FRESH BASIL PASTA: Add 1/4 cup (50 mL) chopped fresh basil to eggs and salt; mix well before incorporating flour.

1 Mound flour on work surface; make well in center. Add eggs and salt to well.

2 Using fork, beat eggs with salt. Starting from inside edge and working around well, gradually incorporate flour into egg mixture until soft dough is formed. Scoop up and sift any flour left on work surface, discarding any bits of dough; set aside.

3 On clean lightly floured surface, knead dough for 10 minutes, working in enough of the sifted flour to make dough smooth and elastic. Cover with plastic wrap and let rest for 20 minutes. Divide dough into 3 pieces to make handling easier; cover.

4 On lightly floured surface, roll out one of the dough pieces into 5-inch (12 cm) long strip; dust with flour. Feed through widest setting of pasta machine rollers 4 times or until edges form smooth line, folding dough in half and lightly flouring after each pass through machine.

5 Set machine to next narrowest setting; run pasta through once without folding. Repeat running dough through rollers until next-to-finest setting is reached, cutting dough in half if awkwardly long. Lightly flour dough; run through finest setting. Repeat with remaining dough.

6 Using pasta rack or broomstick balanced between two chairs, hang dough for 15 to 20 minutes or until leathery but not dry. (If dough dries, remove from rack and pat with damp cloth.)

7 Change setting from rolling to cutting position. Cut pasta into lengths of up to 10 inches (25 cm). Feed each length through cutter. *(Pasta can be covered with plastic wrap and kept at room temperature for up to 1 hour, stored in refrigerator for up to 2 days or frozen for up to 2 months.)* Makes 12 oz (375 g).

Index

Over 100 great new pasta dishes that are fast, flavorful and satisfying.

❦ denotes meatless dish

A
❦ Aglio e Olio, 18
❦ Alfredo - The Classic, 22
❦ Alfredo's Leaner
    Fettuccine, 23
Almonds
    Chicken Curry Pasta, 25
    Curried Chicken Pasta
      Salad, 78
    ❦ Mushroom Tofu
      Noodles, 20
    toasting, 25
Amatriciana, 27
Anchovies
    Broccoli and Rotini
      Salad, 82
    Spaghetti with Walnuts and
      Garlic, 39
    Spinach Fettuccine with
      Cauliflower, 38
    with Penne, 39
Anchovy Paste
    Greek Pasta Salad, 74
Antipasto
    ❦ Fusilli Salad, 74
Artichokes
    and Ham Salad, 76
    ❦ Tomato and Eggplant
      Spaghetti, 12
Asparagus
    ❦ Cannelloni, 60
    New-Style Pasta
      Primavera, 18
    ❦ with Creamy Rotini, 17
    ❦ with Saucy Parmesan
      Pasta, 21

B
Bacon
    Amatriciana, 27
    Creamy Leek Fettuccine, 11
    Minestrone Warm-Up, 40
    Penne with Creamy Tomato
      Sauce, 27
    Spaghetti Carbonara, 30
Basil
    Chicken and Tomato Pasta
      Salad, 78
    Easy Tuna and Garlic
      Pasta, 32

❦ Fresh Pasta, 86
❦ Fresh Tomato and Basil
    Toss, 10
❦ Grilled Vegetable and
    Fusilli Salad, 77
❦ Pack-and-Go Rotini
    Salad, 81
❦ Presto Pesto, 19
❦ Summer-Fresh Pasta, 8
❦ Thai Vegetable Noodles, 85
Bean Sprouts
    Grilled Chicken and Noodle
      Salad, 79
    Pad Thai, 47
Beans
    ❦ Antipasto Fusilli Salad, 74
    Choose-Your-Fish Pasta
      Salad, 75
    Ham and Artichoke Heart
      Salad, 76
    Minestrone Warm-Up, 40

BEEF
    Easy Lasagna, 50
    Fettuccine with Chicken
      Livers, 28
    Fusilli with Meatball
      Stew, 69
    Garden-Fresh Spaghetti, 24
    Pastitsio Pie, 64
    Spaghetti Bolognese, 67
    Spaghetti with Meatballs, 70

Blue Cheese
    ❦ Cheesy Wild Mushroom
      Casserole, 58
    ❦ Gourmand's Gorgonzola
      Linguine, 22
Bows (Bow Ties). *See* **Farfalle**.
Broccoli
    and Rotini Salad, 82
    ❦ Garden Pasta Salad, 76
    Rotini and Clams, 36
    ❦ Sesame Tofu and
      Vegetable Stir-Fry, 48
    Shrimp and Vegetable
      Pasta, 31
Bucatini
    Amatriciana, 27
Buttermilk
    Chicken and Tomato Pasta
      Salad, 78
    Curried Chicken Pasta
      Salad, 78
Butternut Squash
    ❦ Winter Vegetable Pasta
      Toss, 80

C
Cabbage
    Minestrone Warm-Up, 40

CANNELLONI
    ❦ Asparagus, 60
    Cheese and Sausage, 62

Cantaloupe
    Spicy Sesame Noodles, 85
Capellini
    with Smoked Salmon and
      Lemon Cream Sauce, 32
Capers
    ❦ Puttanesca with
      Linguine, 8
Carbonara
    Spaghetti, 30
Carrots
    Curried Chicken Pasta
      Salad, 78
    Fusilli with Meatball
      Stew, 69
    ❦ Garden Pasta Salad, 76
    Lightened-Up Lasagna, 53
    Minestrone Warm-Up, 40
    New-Style Pasta
      Primavera, 18
    ❦ Old-Fashioned Macaroni
      Salad, 80
    ❦ Pesto Spaghetti Salad, 83
    ❦ Sesame Tofu and
      Vegetable Stir-Fry, 48
    ❦ Summer's Fresh Herb
      Tomato Sauce, 71
    ❦ Winter Vegetable Pasta
      Toss, 80
    ❦ Winter's Big-Batch Tomato
      Sauce, 71
    ❦ Zucchini Pasta, 14
Cartwheel-shaped pasta.
    See **Rotelle**.

CASSEROLES
    ❦ Asparagus Cannelloni, 60
    ❦ Baked Chicken and
      Spinach Pasta, 59
    ❦ Baked Vegetable
      Spaghetti, 63
    Cheese and Sausage
      Cannelloni, 62
    ❦ Cheesy Wild Mushroom
      Casserole, 58
    Comfy Macaroni and
      Cheese, 57

Conchiglie with Zucchini and Spinach, 55
Easy Lasagna, 50
freezing, 63
Lightened-Up Lasagna, 53
Macaroni and Cheese Oven Omelette, 62
Macaroni Tomato Pie, 58
Mexican-Style Pork Chop and Spaghetti Bake, 45
Novelle Tuna Casserole, 57
Pastitsio Pie, 64
Seafood and Spinach Lasagna, 52
Tuna Florentine, 56

Cauliflower
Pesto Spaghetti Salad, 83
Spinach Fettuccine with Anchovy Sauce, 38

Cheddar
Cheesy Pasta Frittata, 44
Instant Mac and Cheese, 23
Macaroni and Cheese Oven Omelette, 62
Macaroni Tomato Pie, 58
Macaroni with Four Cheeses, 23
Mexican-Style Pork Chop and Spaghetti Bake, 45
Nouvelle Tuna Casserole, 57
Saucy Pasta, 21

CHEESE
Alfredo's Leaner Fettuccine, 23
Asparagus Cannelloni, 60
Baked Chicken and Spinach Pasta, 59
Baked Vegetable Spaghetti, 63
Cheese and Sausage Cannelloni, 62
Cheesy Chicken Fettuccine, 26
Cheesy Pasta Frittata, 44
Cheesy Wild Mushroom Casserole, 58
Comfy Macaroni and Cheese, 57
Conchiglie with Zucchini and Spinach, 55
Creamy Leek Fettuccine, 11
Creamy Rotini with Asparagus, 17
Easy Lasagna, 50
Farfalle with Ham and Ricotta, 30
Fettuccine Alfredo - The Classic, 22
Garden-Fresh Spaghetti, 24
Gorgonzola Linguine, 22
Greek Pasta Salad, 74
Instant Mac and Cheese, 23
Lightened-Up Lasagna, 53

Linguine with Salmon and Dill, 39
Macaroni and Cheese Oven Omelette, 62
Macaroni Tomato Pie, 58
Macaroni with Four Cheeses, 23
Mexican-Style Pork Chop and Spaghetti Bake, 45
New-Style Pasta Primavera, 18
Nouvelle Tuna Casserole, 57
Old-Fashioned Macaroni Salad, 80
Oodles of Noodles, 10
Pastitsio Pie, 64
Peas, Prosciutto and Tortellini, 29
Red Pepper Herb Pasta, 12
Saucy Parmesan Pasta with Asparagus, 21
Seafood and Spinach Lasagna, 52

Chick-Peas
Antipasto Fusilli Salad, 74
Ditali in Tomato Chick-Pea Sauce, 11
Speedy Tomato and Spinach Soup, 42

CHICKEN
and Noodle Salad, 79
and Spinach Pasta, 59
and Tomato Pasta Salad, 78
Cheesy Fettuccine, 26
Curried Pasta Salad, 78
Curry Pasta, 25
Lightened-Up Lasagna, 53
Fettuccine with Chicken Livers, 28
Livers with Spaghetti and Tomato Sauce, 28
Oriental Stir-Fry Pasta, 26
Starry Stracciatella, 42
Tomato Ragu, 25

Chilies
Mexican-Style Pork Chop and Spaghetti Bake, 45
Chinese. *See* **Oriental.**
Clams
Rotini with Broccoli and Clams, 36
Tomato Clam Pasta, 37
with Spaghetti and Garlic Sauce, 36
Conchiglie
Easy Tuna and Garlic Pasta, 32
Jumbo, with Zucchini and Spinach, 55

Coriander
Buckwheat Noodle Salad, 83
Chicken Curry Pasta, 25
Curried Chicken Pasta Salad, 78
Pad Thai, 47
Spicy Sesame Noodles, 85
Corn
Cheesy Pasta Frittata, 44
Thai Vegetable Noodles, 85
Cottage Cheese
Alfredo's Leaner Fettuccine, 23
Comfy Macaroni and Cheese, 57
Easy Lasagna, 50
Lightened-Up Lasagna, 53
Pastitsio Pie, 64
Cream
Capellini with Smoked Salmon and Lemon Cream Sauce, 32
Creamy Leek Fettuccine, 11
Creamy Rotini with Asparagus, 17
Creamy Scallop Linguine with Vegetables, 35
Fettuccine Alfredo - The Classic, 22
Linguine with Wild Mushroom Sauce, 21
Penne with Creamy Tomato Sauce, 27
Seafood Fettuccine, 35
Cream Cheese
Creamy Leak Fettucine, 11
Oodles of Noodles, 10
Red Pepper Herb Pasta, 12
Cucumber
Buckwheat Noodle Salad, 83
Greek Pasta Salad, 74
Spicy Sesame Noodles, 85
Curry
Chicken Curry Pasta, 25
Curried Chicken Pasta Salad, 78

D
Dill
Old-Fashioned Macaroni Salad, 80
Shrimp and Vegetable Pasta, 31
with Linguine and Salmon, 39
Ditali
in Tomato Chick-Pea Sauce, 11

E
Eggplant
Baked Vegetable Spaghetti, 63
Tomato and Artichoke Spaghetti, 12
Tomato and Whole Wheat Spaghetti, 17
Eggs
Kasha and Bows, 15
Cheesy Pasta Frittata, 44
Conchiglie with Zucchini and Spinach, 55
Easy Lasagna, 50
Macaroni and Cheese Oven Omelette, 62
Pasta Salad Niçoise, 77
Spaghetti Carbonara, 30
Spaghetti Frittata, 45
Starry Stracciatella, 42

F
Farfalle
Greek Pasta Salad, 74
Kasha and Bows, 15
Winter Vegetable Pasta Toss, 80
with Ham and Ricotta, 30
Zucchini Carrot Pasta, 14
Feta
Greek Pasta Salad, 74

FETTUCCINE
Alfredo's Leaner, 23
Alfredo — The Classic, 22
Cheesy Chicken, 26
Chicken Livers, 28
Creamy Leek, 11
Italian Sausage and Tomato, 68
Red Pepper Herb Pasta, 12
Seafood, 35
Spinach with Cauliflower and Anchovy Sauce, 38

FISH. *See also* **SEAFOOD.**
Capellini with Smoked Salmon and Lemon Cream Sauce, 32
Choose-Your-Fish Pasta Salad, 75
Easy Tuna and Garlic Pasta, 32
Linguine with Salmon and Dill, 39
Nouvelle Tuna Casserole, 57
Pasta Salad Niçoise, 77
Seafood and Spinach Lasagna, 52
Tuna Florentine, 56

Fontina Cheese
Cheesy Wild Mushroom Casserole, 58

Frittata
- ❧ Cheesy Pasta, 44
- ❧ Spaghetti, 45

FUSILLI (also Fusilli Lunghi)
- ❧ Antipasto Salad, 74
- ❧ Cheesy Pasta Frittata, 44
- ❧ Grilled Vegetable Salad, 77
- Italian Sausage and Tomato, 68
- New-Style Pasta Primavera, 18
- Nouvelle Tuna Casserole, 57
- ❧ Oodles of Noodles, 10
- Pasta Salad Niçoise, 77
- ❧ Saucy Parmesan Pasta with Asparagus, 21
- with Meatball Stew, 69
- with Mussels, 33

G

Garlic
- ❧ Aglio e Olio, 18
- Easy Tuna and Garlic Pasta, 32
- ❧ Presto Pesto, 19
- Spaghetti with Anchovies, Walnuts and Garlic, 39
- Spaghetti with Fast Clam and Garlic Sauce, 36

Goat Cheese (Chèvre)
- ❧ Asparagus Cannelloni, 60
- ❧ Creamy Rotini with Asparagus, 17

Gorgonzola
- ❧ Cheesy Wild Mushroom Casserole, 58
- ❧ Gourmand's Linguine, 22

Greek
- Pasta Salad, 74

Green Beans
- Ham and Artichoke Heart Salad, 76

Green Onions
- ❧ Asparagus Cannelloni, 60
- Choose-Your-Fish Pasta Salad, 75
- Curried Chicken Pasta Salad, 78
- Ham and Artichoke Heart Salad, 76
- Lightened-Up Lasagna, 53
- Linguine with Salmon and Dill, 39
- ❧ Old-Fashioned Macaroni Salad, 80
- Pad Thai, 47
- ❧ Sesame Tofu and Vegetable Stir-Fry, 48
- Spicy Sesame Noodles, 85
- ❧ Thai Vegetable Noodles, 85
- ❧ Winter Vegetable Pasta Toss, 80

Gruyère
- ❧ Macaroni with Four Cheeses, 23

H

Ham. *See also* **Prosciutto.**
- and Artichoke Heart Salad, 76
- Baked Chicken and Spinach Pasta, 59
- Comfy Macaroni and Cheese, 57
- Peas, Prosciutto and Tortellini, 29
- with Farfalle and Ricotta, 30

Herbs. *See also* **Basil, Coriander, Dill, Oregano.**
- Red Pepper Herb Pasta, 12
- ❧ Summer's Fresh Tomato Sauce, 71
- ❧ Winter's Big-Batch Tomato Sauce, 71

Hoisin
- Spicy Sesame Noodles, 85
- ❧ Thai Vegetable Noodles, 85

I

INFORMATION
- asparagus - cleaning, 60
- casseroles - freezing, 63
- cheeses for pasta, 22
- hot pepper flakes, 53
- leeks - cleaning, 11
- make-ahead minestrone, 40
- meat sauces - storing, 66
- mussels - buying and preparing, 32
- olive oil, 19
- olives, 14
- pancetta, 27
- pasta - choosing the best, 27
- pasta - cooking, back flap
- pasta - checking for doneness, back flap
- pasta - how much?, back flap
- pasta - pairing with sauces, 68
- pasta, serving, back flap
- pasta - stocking the cupboard, 36
- pasta - storing, 28
- pasta shells (conchiglie) - stuffing, 55
- pesto - thinning, 19
- salad add-ins, 76
- sausage with fennel seeds, 68
- spinach - cooking, 52
- substitutes - fresh tomatoes for sun-dried, 14
- substitutes - prosciutto, pancetta, Calabrian sausages, 66
- Thai ingredients, 47

- toasting almonds, 25
- toasting peanuts, 25
- toasting sesame seeds, 85
- tofu, 48
- tomatoes - canning, 72
- tomatoes - for sauce, 70
- tomatoes - storing, 10

K

Kasha
- ❧ and Bows, 15

L

LASAGNA
- Cheese and Sausage Cannelloni, 62
- Easy, 50
- Lightened-Up, 53

Leeks
- cleaning, 11
- Creamy Fettuccine, 11

Lemons
- Capellini with Smoked Salmon, 32
- ❧ Asparagus Cannelloni, 60

LINGUINE
- ❧ Alfredo's Leaner, 23
- Creamy Leek, 11
- Creamy Scallop, with Vegetables, 35
- ❧ Gourmand's Gorgonzola, 22
- Puttanesca, 8
- Seafood, 35
- Shrimp and Vegetable Pasta, 31
- ❧ Summer-Fresh Pasta, 8
- Tomato and Wild Mushroom, 67
- with Mussels, 33
- with Salmon and Dill, 39
- ❧ with Wild Mushroom Sauce, 21

Lobster
- Seafood and Spinach Lasagna, 52

M

MACARONI
- ❧ and Cheese Oven Omelette, 62
- Comfy Macaroni and Cheese, 57
- ❧ in Tomato Chick-Pea Sauce, 11
- ❧ Instant Mac and Cheese, 23
- ❧ Kasha and Bows, 15
- Minestrone Warm-Up, 40

- ❧ Old-Fashioned Salad, 80
- ❧ Oodles of Noodles, 10
- Pastitsio Pie, 64
- ❧ Tomato Pie, 58
- ❧ with Four Cheeses, 23

Mexican
- Pork Chop and Spaghetti Bake, 45

Monkfish
- Seafood and Spinach Lasagna, 52

MOZZARELLA
- ❧ Asparagus Cannelloni, 60
- Baked Chicken and Spinach Pasta, 59
- ❧ Baked Vegetable Spaghetti, 63
- Cheese and Sausage Cannelloni, 62
- Cheesy Chicken Fettuccine, 26
- Comfy Macaroni and Cheese, 57
- Easy Lasagna, 50
- Garden-Fresh Spaghetti, 24
- ❧ Lightened-Up Lasagna, 53
- ❧ Macaroni with Four Cheeses, 23
- ❧ Old-Fashioned Macaroni Salad, 80
- Seafood and Spinach Lasagna, 52

MUSHROOMS
- ❧ Cheesy Wild Mushroom Casserole, 58
- ❧ Buckwheat Noodle Salad, 83
- ❧ Cheesy Pasta Frittata, 44
- Creamy Scallop Linguine with Vegetables, 35
- ❧ Ditali in Tomato Chick-Pea Sauce, 11
- ❧ Fast and Easy Spaghetti Sauce, 70
- Fusilli with Meatball Stew, 69
- ❧ Grilled Vegetable and Fusilli Salad, 77
- Italian Sausage and Tomato Fettuccine, 68
- Oriental Stir-Fry Pasta, 26
- ❧ Sesame Tofu and Vegetable Stir-Fry, 48
- ❧ Summer-Fresh Pasta, 8
- ❧ Tofu Noodles, 20
- ❧ Tomato Linguine, 67
- ❧ with Linguine and Sauce, 21

Mussels
- buying and preparing, 32
- Seafood Fettuccine, 35
- with Fusilli, 33

N

Noodles, Buckwheat Noodles (Soba) and Rice Noodles
- Buckwheat Noodle Salad, 83
- Grilled Chicken and Noodle Salad, 79
- Mushroom Tofu Noodles, 20
- Oriental Shrimp Noodle Soup, 42
- Pad Thai, 47
- Spicy Sesame Noodles, 85
- Tuna Florentine, 56

O

OLIVE OIL
- Aglio e Olio, 18
- Antipasto Fusilli Salad, 74
- Broccoli and Rotini Salad, 82
- Conchiglie with Zucchini and Spinach, 55
- Easy Tuna and Garlic Pasta, 32
- extra virgin, 19
- Fettuccine with Chicken Livers, 28
- Fresh Tomato and Basil Toss, 10
- Greek Pasta Salad, 74
- Grilled Vegetable and Fusilli Salad, 77
- Ham and Artichoke Heart Salad, 76
- Penne with Swiss Chard, Raisins and Pine Nuts, 16
- Presto Pesto, 19
- Pack-and-Go Rotini Salad, 81
- Spaghetti with Anchovies, Walnuts and Garlic, 39
- Olive and Sun-Dried Tomato Spaghettini, 14
- Summer-Fresh Pasta, 8
- varieties, 19

OLIVES
- buying, 14
- Choose-Your-Fish Pasta Salad, 75
- Creamy Rotini with Asparagus, 17
- Greek Pasta Salad, 74
- Pasta Salad Niçoise, 77
- Puttanesca with Linguine, 8
- Olive and Sun-Dried Tomato Spaghettini, 14
- Tomato, Eggplant and Artichoke Spaghetti, 12
- varieties, 14

Onions. *See also* **Green Onions.**
- Zucchini Carrot Pasta, 14
- Creamy Rotini with Asparagus, 17
- Farfalle with Ham and Ricotta, 30
- Greek Pasta Salad, 74
- Kasha and Bows, 15
- Mushroom Tofu Noodles, 20
- Saucy Parmesan Pasta with Asparagus, 21

Oriental
- Buckwheat Noodle Salad, 83
- Grilled Chicken and Noodle Salad, 79
- Mushroom Tofu Noodles, 20
- Pad Thai, 47
- Sesame Tofu and Vegetable Stir-Fry, 48
- Shrimp Noodle Soup, 42
- Spicy Sesame Noodles, 85
- Stir-Fry Pasta, 26
- Thai Vegetable Noodles, 85

P

Pad Thai, 47

Pancetta
- Amatriciana, 27
- definition, 27
- Minestrone Warm-Up, 40
- Penne with Creamy Tomato Sauce, 27
- Spaghetti Carbonara, 30
- substitute, 66

PARMESAN
- Abruzzi-Style Spaghetti, 66
- Alfredo's Leaner Fettuccine, 23
- Amatriciana, 27
- Baked Chicken and Spinach Pasta, 59
- cheeses for pasta, 22
- Cheesy Chicken Fettuccine, 26
- Cheesy Wild Mushroom Casserole, 58
- Conchiglie with Zucchini and Spinach, 55
- Easy Lasagna, 50
- Farfalle with Ham and Ricotta, 30
- Fettuccine Alfredo - The Classic, 22
- Fettuccine with Chicken Livers, 28
- Gourmand's Gorgonzola Linguine, 22
- Macaroni with Four Cheeses, 23
- Pasta with Asparagus, 21
- Pastitsio Pie, 64

- Presto Pesto, 19
- Red Pepper Herb Pasta, 12
- Rotini with Broccoli and Clams, 36
- Seafood and Spinach Lasagna, 52
- Spaghetti Carbonara, 30
- Spaghetti Frittata, 45
- Zucchini Carrot Pasta, 14

Parmigiano Reggiano. *See* **PARMESAN.**

Parsley
- Aglio e Olio, 18
- Fusilli with Mussels, 33
- Seafood Fettuccine, 35
- Spaghetti with Fast Clam and Garlic Sauce, 36

PASTA
- amounts fresh and dried, 29
- choosing pasta, 27
- checking for doneness, back flap
- cooking times, back flap
- how to make fresh, 86
- portions, back flap
- serving, back flap
- stocking the cupboard, 36
- storage, 28

Pastitsio
- Pie, 64

Peanuts
- Chicken Curry Pasta, 25
- Grilled Chicken and Noodle Salad, 79
- Pad Thai, 47
- toasting, 25

Peas. *See also* **Snow Peas.**
- Capellini with Smoked Salmon and Lemon Cream Sauce, 32
- Cheesy Chicken Fettuccine, 26
- Cheesy Pasta Frittata, 44
- Fusilli with Meatball Stew, 69
- New-Style Pasta Primavera, 18
- Prosciutto and Tortellini, 29
- Starry Stracciatella, 42

PENNE
- and Broccoli Salad, 82
- Baked Chicken and Spinach Pasta, 59
- Chicken and Tomato Pasta Salad, 78
- Creamy, with Asparagus, 17
- Chicken Curry Pasta, 25
- Fresh Tomato and Basil Toss, 10

- Ham and Artichoke Heart Salad, 76
- in Tomato Chick-Pea Sauce, 11
- Nouvelle Tuna Casserole, 57
- Pasta Salad Niçoise, 77
- with Anchovy Sauce, 39
- with Creamy Tomato Sauce, 27
- with Sausage and Tomato, 29
- with Swiss Chard, Raisins and Pine Nuts, 16

PEPPERS
- Arrabbiata, 10
- Baked Chicken and Spinach Pasta, 59
- Baked Vegetable Spaghetti, 63
- Choose-Your-Fish Pasta Salad, 75
- Curried Chicken Pasta Salad, 78
- Fast and Easy Spaghetti Sauce, 70
- Fettuccine with Chicken Livers, 28
- Fusilli with Meatball Stew, 69
- Garden Pasta Salad, 76
- Garden-Fresh Spaghetti, 24
- Grilled Vegetable and Fusilli Salad, 77
- Italian Sausage and Tomato Fettuccine, 68
- Lightened-Up Lasagna, 53
- New-Style Pasta Primavera, 18
- Old-Fashioned Macaroni Salad, 80
- Oriental Stir-Fry Pasta, 26
- Pack-and Go Rotini Salad, 81
- Pad Thai, 47
- Pasta Salad Niçoise, 77
- Penne with Sausage and Tomato, 29
- Pesto Spaghetti Salad, 83
- Red Pepper Herb Pasta, 12
- Roasted Red Pepper Pasta, 86
- Shrimp and Vegetable Pasta, 31
- Skillet Turkey and Pasta Supper, 48
- Thai Vegetable Noodles, 85
- Winter's Big Batch Tomato Sauce, 71

PESTO
- Parsley, 40
- Presto, 19
- Spaghetti Salad, 83
- thinning, 19

Pine Nuts
Broccoli and Rotini
Salad, 82
Minestrone Warm-Up, 40
❧ Penne with Swiss Chard
and Raisins, 16
❧ Presto Pesto, 19
Porcini Mushrooms
❧ Linguine with Wild
Mushroom Sauce, 21

PORK. *See also* **bacon, ham,
pancetta, prosciutto, sausage**.
Chops and Mexican-Style
Spaghetti Bake, 45
Abruzzi-Style Spaghetti, 66
Pad Thai, 47

Potatoes
Minestrone Warm-Up, 40
Prosciutto
Peas and Tortellini, 29
substitute, 66
Tomato and Wild Mushroom
Linguine, 67
Provolone
Cheesy Chicken
Fettuccine, 26
Puttanesca
❧ with Linguine, 8

R
Radiatore
Curried Chicken Pasta
Salad, 78
Radishes
❧ Buckwheat Noodle
Salad, 83
Raisins
Broccoli and Rotini
Salad, 82
Chicken Curry Pasta, 25
❧ with Swiss Chard, Pine
Nuts and Penne, 16
Red Onions. *See* **Onions.**
Rice Vermicelli
Oriental Shrimp Noodle
Soup, 42
❧ Sesame Tofu and
Vegetable Stir-Fry, 48

RICOTTA
❧ Asparagus Cannelloni, 60
Cheese and Sausage
Cannelloni, 62
❧ Conchiglie with Zucchini
and Spinach, 55
Linguine with Salmon and
Dill, 39
Peas, Prosciutto and
Tortellini, 29
with Farfalle and Ham, 30

Rigatoni
❧ Cheesy Wild Mushroom
Casserole, 58
Rotelle
❧ Garden Pasta Salad, 76

ROTINI
and Broccoli Salad, 82
Choose-Your-Fish Pasta
Salad, 75
Easy Tuna and Garlic
Pasta, 32
❧ Fresh Tomato and Basil
Toss, 10
Minestrone Warm-Up, 40
❧ Pack-and-Go Salad, 81
Skillet Turkey and Pasta
Supper, 48
Tomato Clam Pasta, 37
❧ Tomato, Chick-Pea and
Spinach Soup, 42
❧ with Asparagus, 17
with Broccoli and Clams, 36

Rutabaga
❧ Winter Vegetable Pasta
Toss, 80

S
Saffron
❧ Pasta, 86

SALADS
❧ Antipasto Fusilli, 74
Broccoli and Rotini, 82
❧ Buckwheat Noodle, 83
Chicken and Tomato
Pasta, 78
Choose-Your-Fish Pasta, 75
Curried Chicken Pasta, 78
❧ Garden Pasta, 76
Greek Pasta, 74
Grilled Chicken and
Noodle, 79
❧ Grilled Vegetable and
Fusilli, 77
Ham and Artichoke, 76
❧ Old-Fashioned
Macaroni, 80
❧ Pack-and-Go Rotini, 81
Pasta Niçoise, 77
❧ Pesto Spaghetti, 83
Spicy Sesame Noodles, 85
❧ Thai Vegetable Noodles, 85
❧ Winter Vegetable Pasta
Toss, 80

Salmon
Capellini with Smoked
Salmon and Lemon Cream
Sauce, 32
Choose-Your-Fish Pasta
Salad, 75
Salsa
❧ Pack-and-Go Rotini
Salad, 81

SAUCES
Abruzzi-Style Spaghetti, 66
Creamy Tomato, 27
❧ Fast and Easy Spaghetti, 70
Fusilli with Meatball
Stew, 69
Italian Sausage and Tomato
Fettuccine, 68
❧ Presto Pesto, 19
Spaghetti Bolognese, 67
Spaghetti with Meatballs, 70
storing meat sauces, 66
❧ Summer's Fresh Herb
Tomato Sauce, 71
Tomato and Wild Mushroom
Linguine, 67
tomatoes for, 70
❧ Winter's Big-Batch
Tomato, 71

Sausages
Calabrian substitute, 66
Abruzzi-Style Spaghetti, 66
Italian Sausage and Tomato
Fettuccine, 68
Cheese Cannelloni, 62
Easy Lasagna, 50
with Penne and Tomato, 29
Scallops. *See* **SEAFOOD.**

SEAFOOD. *See also* **FISH.**
Creamy Scallop Linguine
with Vegetables, 35
Fusilli with Mussels, 33
Oriental Shrimp Noodle
Soup, 42
Pad Thai, 47
Rotini with Broccoli and
Clams, 36
Seafood and Spinach
Lasagna, 52
Shrimp and Vegetable
Pasta, 31
Seafood Fettuccine, 35
Spaghetti with Fast Clam
and Garlic Sauce, 36
Tomato Clam Pasta, 37

Sesame seeds
Spicy Noodles, 85
Thai Vegetable Noodles, 85
toasting, 85
Shells. *See* **Conchiglie.**

Shrimp
and Vegetable Pasta, 31
Oriental Shrimp Noodle
Soup, 42
Pad Thai, 47
Seafood Fettuccine, 35
Seafood and Spinach
Lasagna, 52
Smoked Salmon
with Lemon Cream Sauce
and Capellini, 32
with Linguine and Dill, 39
Snow Peas
Chicken and Tomato Pasta
Salad, 78
Grilled Chicken and Noodle
Salad, 79
Oriental Shrimp Noodle
Soup, 42
Oriental Stir-Fry Pasta, 26
❧ Thai Vegetable Noodles, 85
Soba (Buckwheat Noodles)
❧ Buckwheat Noodle
Salad, 83
Grilled Chicken and Noodle
Salad, 79
Sole
Seafood and Spinach
Lasagna, 52

SOUPS
make-ahead, 40
Minestrone Warm-Up, 40
Oriental Shrimp Noodle, 42
❧ Speedy Tomato, Chick-Pea
and Spinach Soup, 42
Starry Stracciatella, 42

SPAGHETTI
Abruzzi-Style, 66
❧ Aglio e Olio, 18
❧ Arrabbiata, 10
❧ Baked Vegetable, 63
Bolognese, 67
Carbonara, 30
Chicken Livers and
Tomatoes, 28
Chicken Curry Pasta, 25
❧ Fast and Easy Sauce, 70
❧ Frittata, 45
Garden-Fresh, 24
Grilled Chicken and Noodle
Salad, 79
Mexican-Style Pork Chop
Bake, 45
❧ Mushroom Tofu
Noodles, 20
❧ Pesto Salad, 83
Shrimp and Vegetable
Pasta, 31
❧ Summer-Fresh Pasta, 8
❧ Thai Vegetable Noodles, 85
❧ Tomato, Eggplant and
Artichoke, 12
Very Tomato and Chicken
Ragu, 25